# GAME OF MY LIFE

## KENTUCKY

# WILDCATS

MEMORABLE STORIES OF WILDCATS BASKETBALL

## RYAN CLARK

SPORTS
PUBLISHING

For Mom, who has always been there.

For Granddad, who got to me first.

For Manda, who lets me have this obsession of mine.

Sports Publishing books may be purchased in bulk at special discounts for sales promotion, corporate gifts, fund-raising, or educational purposes. Special editions can also be created to specifications. For details, contact the Special Sales Department, Sports Publishing, 307 West 36th Street, 11th Floor, New York, NY 10018 or sportspubbooks@ skyhorsepublishing.com.

Sports Publishing® is a registered trademark of Skyhorse Publishing, Inc.®, a Delaware corporation.

Visit our website at www.sportspubbooks.com

10 9 8 7 6 5 4 3 2 1

Library of Congress Cataloging-in-Publication Data is available on file.

ISBN: 978-1-61321-051-2

Printed in the United States of America

# CONTENTS

Foreword ........................................ v

Introduction ................................... vii

RALPH BEARD ................................. 1

FRANK RAMSEY ............................... 9

VERNON HATTON ............................. 17

COTTON NASH ............................... 25

LOUIE DAMPIER ............................. 31

DAN ISSEL ................................... 37

MIKE FLYNN ................................. 43

KEVIN GREVEY .............................. 49

RICK ROBEY ................................. 57

KYLE MACY .................................. 63

JACK GIVENS ................................ 69

SAM BOWIE .................................. 77

KENNY WALKER .............................. 85

JOHN PELPHREY ............................. 93

REGGIE HANSON ............................ 101

RICHIE FARMER ............................. 107

JAMAL MASHBURN .......................... 117

AMINU TIMBERLAKE ........................ 125

TODD SVOBODA ............................. 133

TRAVIS FORD ................................. 141

WALTER McCARTY ............................ 149

TONY DELK .................................. 157

DEREK ANDERSON ........................... 165

CAMERON MILLS ............................ 173

ALLEN EDWARDS ............................ 181

SCOTT PADGETT ............................ 189

JEFF SHEPPARD ............................. 199

TAYSHAUN PRINCE .......................... 207

PATRICK SPARKS ............................ 215

RAJON RONDO ............................... 223

PATRICK PATTERSON ........................ 231

BRANDON KNIGHT ........................... 237

JOSH HARRELLSON ......................... 243

ACKNOWLEDGMENTS ........................ 247

# FOREWORD

Dick Vitale has seen the best and worst of Kentucky basketball. He watched as the program succeeded and then suffered through the lean years of the late 1980s probation. Then he watched in the 1990s as the Wildcats came back to reclaim their spot among the nation's elite teams.

"Everyone knows there are few teams like Kentucky," Vitale says.

For more than 25 years Vitale has broadcast basketball games on ESPN and ABC. He admits Rupp Arena is one of his favorite places. But of course, one game was different from the rest.

February 4, 2003. Lexington. The Florida Gators, led by standouts Matt Bonner, Anthony Roberson, Matt Walsh, David Lee and Brett Nelson, came to Rupp Arena with a No. 1 ranking—the first time the school's basketball program could boast of that distinction. Roberson told reporters beforehand he was unafraid of the Rupp Arena atmosphere. A columnist for the Orlando Sentinel newspaper predicted Florida would use the game to overtake Kentucky as the dominant team in the SEC.

That night, ESPN commentators joined 24,459 fans to become the largest crowd ever to see Kentucky play a game in Rupp Arena. They loved what they saw. Erik Daniels, Chuck Hayes, Marquis Estill, Gerald Fitch, Keith Bogans, and Cliff Hawkins led the charge.

The game was close in the early minutes, with sixth-ranked Kentucky clinging to a 15-14 lead. But a late 22-2 run, filled with high-flying dunks and steals, created a 45-22 halftime bulge.

"This is humiliation! Jam City! It's an embarrassment!" Vitale said that night on the air. "This is a fastbreak layup drill. This is embarrassing for No.1."

The 70-55 victory looked much closer than it actually was, as Florida never mounted a serious run in the second half and were down by as many as 29 points. Kentucky's team effort produced 19 assists on its 30 field goals and set the tone for the rest of the season's 26-game winning streak en route to the NCAA Tournament's overall No. 1 seed.

But it was that night in February when the nation first saw the 2003 UK squad flex its muscles against the No. 1 Gators. Those who were there say the crowd was unlike any they've ever heard.

# THE (UK) GAME OF MY LIFE
## NO. 6 KENTUCKY 70, NO. 1 FLORIDA 55
### FEBRUARY 4, 2003
#### BY DICK VITALE

There's been so many great games I've covered involving the University of Kentucky, baby. The fans just go bananas there in Lexington. To pick just one game is so difficult, there have been so many good ones that I've been able to see. From Joe B. Hall to Eddie Sutton to Rick Pitino and Tubby, there are more great moments than I can remember.

But of all the games there is one that stands out. Kentucky and Florida. The Wildcats and the Gators—2003. That was a great rivalry then like it is now, and that was the first time Billy Donovan's team had ever been ranked No. 1—in the history of Florida basketball! But they came into a frenzied atmosphere in Lexington that day. The Cats were ready.

Tubby Smith had those guys so ready to play, from the opening tip. I mean, Florida was No. 1—everybody's bulletin-board material. You want to beat No. 1. But Kentucky did more than beat that team. They flat-out dominated Florida.

I've been to Rupp Arena many times in my career, but I've never heard it as electric as it was that night. From the very beginning, that Kentucky team got after it defensively, and that became the mark of that team. It's a team that, looking back, was very, very talented, with players like Fitch and Bogans and Chuck Hayes.

But they got up early in the first half and the fans went absolutely crazy. And I know they fed off that energy. By the second half, it was no contest, baby. It was dipsy-doo, dunkeroo time. Kentucky absolutely ran away with it, and Florida's No. 1 ranking was gone. And those fans in Lexington just ate it up. Some people thought the Gators might come into Rupp and beat the Cats. Didn't happen.

It's a tough question—the best UK game you've ever seen—but I'd have to say that was the biggest I've been a part of. I know there will be more.

# INTRODUCTION

Every October, when the basketball season begins, the whispers echo from the hills of Harlan to the city parks of Louisville. How is the team this year? Will they be any good? Will they make the Final Four? And it all leads up to that first tip, when the game begins and the crowd can see the team with their own eyes. And the boys are perfect—they can run and jump and shoot with any team in the country. It's as beautiful as ballet, if you've seen a ballet. The Wildcats are magic, and for a state like Kentucky, we need a little magic every once and a while.

I grew up in this culture, loving the Big Blue. For those north of the Mason-Dixon, that's the Kentucky Wildcats basketball team. It was my Granddad that showed me the light, as he says. He got to me before my Daddy could. Daddy cheered for the hometown Louisville Cardinals, which to Granddad was just about as sinful as treading your dirty shoes on the carpet, or leaving your garbage anywhere but in the wastebasket.

And when Daddy died when I was little, the bond between Granddad and me grew. We'd watch the basketball games together. It became our shared time, the time we had when no one else could interfere.

To Granddad and me, the game means so much. It defines who we are, and it makes up a large part of our relationship.

I still root for the Big Blue. Because whatever the reason, rooting for Kentucky stays with a person. Like a shadow. Or a good memory. It's something few understand. In a state with so much sports history—the Kentucky Derby, Muhammad Ali, Johnny Unitas, Paul Hornung, Pee Wee Reese—there has always been someone to root for. But there are no professional sports teams. And of those teams closest to us, in Indianapolis or Cincinnati or Nashville, none are perennial winners. Not like Kentucky basketball.

As I try to explain to people who are not sports fans, Kentuckians can only call themselves "the best" in a few categories. Much too often, the state falls to the bottom in the statistics of literacy, education, teen pregnancy, or job growth. And for all these faults, we are a proud people, and we search for things to be proud of. Thankfully, there's always been the Wildcats.

I've found that those who don't know much about Kentucky still know about the college basketball team and its long history of excellence. If we as a state have nothing else, we still have the Big Blue, and it is this tradition into which I was born. I took to it like a kid at Christmas. And years later, even after attending another state university, I still couldn't shake my love for Kentucky basketball. I didn't want to.

Together, Granddad and I have seen a lot. We've watched national championships, dramatic comebacks, and we've seen our share of losses, too. We've gotten angry together, and we've screamed and celebrated until we were hoarse. It's our thing, our tradition. It's what we share. It is our passion.

And I'm proud to say the Game of My Life, or at least the most enjoyable game I have seen in person was with him, and it's chronicled in this book. Look for it in the chapter on Richie Farmer. Granddad and I watched many of these games on television while sitting on the couch at home. You probably did, too.

Enjoy reliving them with your heroes. Listen to their greatest games in their voices. And be proud. All over again.

Go Big Blue.

Ryan Clark
April 2007

# CHAPTER 1

# RALPH BEARD

From the earliest years of his life, Ralph Beard loved basketball. Beard's mother, Sue, recalls her son's unusual propensity for the sport. As an infant, Ralph would throw a rubber ball into his potty chair. Then the Beards nailed a hoop above his bed; and then the hoop went above the kitchen door. Finally, Ralph started playing on a normal hoop outside. There he crafted his shot and worked on his ball handling.

After winning a state championship at Louisville Male High School in 1945, he told Coach Adolph Rupp he wanted to play guard at Kentucky.

"Ralph Beard is the greatest basketball player I ever saw," said Rupp, as quoted by sportscaster Denny Trease. "When Beard ran, you could smell the rubber burning."

Cat quick, Beard could score and defend, making him a perfect fit for Rupp's fast-paced teams. There was only one problem: Beard accepted a football scholarship from then-football coach Bernie Shively. In his first game, though, the halfback separated both shoulders, effectively ending his football career. "I think to this day football could've been my best sport," Beard says. "I wanted to play everything at Kentucky. I was so fast I think I could have been a really, really good football player."

Instead, he focused on basketball, and Kentucky fans are forever grateful.

# THE SETTING

Bill Keightley, Kentucky's equipment manager since the 1950s, is just one of a long line of former Kentucky greats to say that Beard was talented enough to have played and been effective even in today's game.

Keightley was in high school at the same time as Beard, and he remembers watching some of Beard's games at the old Alumni Gym. "His hands were so quick, and he handled the ball so well," Keightley recalls. "He would definitely have had an impact on today's game. I think you could put him in games right now and he'd be impressive."

When Beard joined UK's basketball team in 1945, Kentucky had not won a national championship in Rupp's 16 years as coach—although the team had visited the Final Four and participated in the NIT. But from 1943 to 1945, the Wildcats had established themselves as the class of the SEC, winning two regular-season championships and two tournament titles. Backed by the scoring of center Alex Groza and forward Jack Tingle, the Wildcats seemed to be on the cusp of capturing their first national championship.

Enter Ralph Beard, along with Harlan's own Wah Wah Jones, who would help change Kentucky basketball forever.

* * *

In 1946, when Jones and Beard joined the Wildcats, the team posted an impressive 28-2 record, including 6-0 in the SEC. The only losses came by eight points to Temple and by nine points to Notre Dame. The next step was the National Invitational Tournament, the Granddaddy of the postseason tournaments in that era.

"The NCAA was more like YMCA at the time," Beard says. "Everyone wanted to be a part of the NIT at the time. It was the big, big tournament, and that's where you set your sights." In the NIT, the most skilled teams in the country were invited to Madison Square Garden to play in the best of tournaments—and it was clear that was the Wildcats' goal.

Kentucky dispatched Arizona in their first-round game, 77-53, and then downed West Virginia, 59-51. In the championship game, Kentucky faced Rhode Island, an underdog according to experts of

---

Ralph Beard hit the game-winning free throw to clinch Kentucky's first national championship.

2

the day. But Rhode Island had All-American Ernie Calverley on its roster. Many wondered if one All-American from Rhode Island could create enough offense to keep up with the high-powered Wildcats attack. Kentucky, which entered as an 11 1/2-point favorite, was supposed to win big.

"Rhode Island . . . was not supposed to be equipped with the defense necessary to stop . . . Kentucky," wrote Louis Effrat, of The *New York Times*. "[The Rhode Island offense,] with its electrifying one-handers, had been subjected to ridicule and certainly did not compare with Kentucky's orthodox offense, revolving around the pivot man."

But like many college basketball games, nothing went according to plan.

# THE GAME OF MY LIFE
## NIT CHAMPIONSHIP:
### KENTUCKY 46, RHODE ISLAND 45
### MARCH 20, 1946
### BY RALPH BEARD

It's almost impossible for me to choose one game as The Game of My Life. Three out of the four years I was at Kentucky, we won national championships. We were all pioneers, doing these things for the first time.

But in 1946, we won the first national championship for Kentucky. The NIT, like I said, was the big tournament. You wanted to be one of those eight teams invited to New York.

As a freshman, I was only 17 years old, and I didn't really understand the pressure of playing in a national championship game yet. But I guess I played OK. I scored some points, and I had to play defense on [Calverley], so I was busy all night.

At first it seemed like the game was going to go like everyone thought. We were up [23-16], but then they went on a big run, making a lot of shots to go up [Rhode Island led 27-26 at the half]. We knew we just had to play our kind of basketball.

In the second half, it just went back and forth, and we couldn't shake them. But we made some big plays down the stretch, and I found myself on the free-throw line with under a minute to go to break the tie. You didn't want to think too much about it—that this was the free throw that could win Kentucky its first championship.

So I shot it up.

I made the winning free throw, and at 17 years old, I didn't realize the importance of it. I'm sure I was nervous, but the Good Lord gave me the good fortune to roll it in.

That was the first championship for us. And afterward, that was the first time I saw Coach Rupp dance a little jig. And he did—right there, after we got the trophy. He was always a bit stoic, but he knew how important that was. That meant a lot. That set the tone for all the history to come.

**Statline:**

| FG | FT | PTS |
|----|----|-----|
| 5 | 3 | 13 |

# THE RESULT

After 12 ties and 11 lead changes, Kentucky won its first championship on a free throw by its precocious freshman Ralph Beard, who led his team with 13 points. Wah Wah Jones contributed 10 points, and Beard held Calverley to eight points. The *Times* noted Beard's overall play, declaring him "Kentucky's standout offensively and defensively."

But the final minutes were wrought with tension. With two minutes remaining, Kentucky trailed 45-44. Then, Calverley fouled Kentucky center Kenton Campbell, who made a free throw to tie the game.

With 40 seconds to go, Calverley fouled again, his fifth foul of the game. This time it was Beard who went to the line and converted the winning point for the final margin. Rhode Island missed a free throw, which would have tied the game, and then failed to get off a clean shot in the game's final possession.

"Who said Rhode Island had no defense?" Rupp angrily asked the *Times* after the game. "Who said Rhode Island had no offense?" Rhode Island had fought hard and won fans for its gutsy play against the more talented Wildcats. But it was Kentucky that, on that day, started what would later be known as its first dynasty.

\* \* \*

Beard rose to basketball stardom as a three-time All-American who would win an NCAA Championship in 1948 and another in

1949. He was featured on the cover of the first issue of *Sports Illustrated* in 1948 under the headline: "Ralph Beard: Fiery guard who is helping Kentucky defend its title in basketball."

The 1948 Wildcats squad, which successfully defended its title, would become known as one of the best lineups in the history of basketball. All five starters participated in the 1948 Olympics in London, where they swept eight games and won the gold medal.

"We didn't have that much competition," Beard says. "We were so far ahead of the world at that time. I don't want to brag, but that's the way it was." Excluding a close 59-57 victory over Argentina, no other team came within 25 points of the Kentucky stars.

After the 1949 season, Rupp honored the seniors who led Kentucky to three national titles by hanging their jerseys from the rafters of the gymnasium. Cliff Barker, Alex Groza, Wah Wah Jones, Kenny Rollins, and Ralph Beard would always be remembered as the "Fabulous Five." The nickname stuck when Rupp said no team would ever again play as "fabulous" as that team.

* * *

Following his senior year, Beard was selected by Chicago in the second round of the NBA Draft. "But the NBA was fledgling," Beard says. "So we said, 'Let's start our own team.'" That's how the Indianapolis Olympians came into being. Beard led a roster of skilled Kentucky players. By his second season he would be an All-NBA performer.

Then the fallout occurred, and Beard would never be the same again. He confessed to accepting $500 from gamblers while he was playing at Kentucky—although he contends he never altered the outcome of any games. He was banned from basketball after just two years of NBA play. In two seasons, he averaged 15.9 points, and by his second year, he was an all-star and an All-NBA first-teamer. After the scandal, his career was over.

"The Lord knows I never did anything to influence any games," Beard says. "I'd never had money, and I was blinded by it. But I never did fix any games." It was an allegation Beard spent his entire life living down.

"Well, you can just give up, or you can keep fighting," Beard says. "You've got to go on. You've got to keep living. I had to move on."

# AFTER BLUE

For years, Beard would continue playing in amateur leagues, where company workers would tell tales of the day they took the court against—or with—the legendary Ralph Beard. "I love basketball," he says. "And I loved to play."

He doesn't talk much of the things he lost because of his too-brief professional career. He could've made huge sums of money. He could've been one of the legends of the NBA. He could've been inducted into basketball's Hall of Fame. But as he says, one cannot dwell on these things; one must move on.

Now Beard is retired, living in Louisville with his wife, where he enjoys talking to fans and watching basketball games. He still loves golf, although it's become difficult to play since he developed polymyositis, which causes pain in his muscles.

In his basement, he has trophies and newspaper clippings—and a copy of his old *Sports Illustrated* cover magazine. He's even got a parchment certificate and medal he received from the Olympics—an event that he says he was only lucky enough to attend because his mother saved up money for him to go.

"I can't thank her enough," Beard says today. "My dad left us when I was little, and she worked so hard to give me money so I could go over to the Olympics. She was wonderful."

When his basketball career was over, Beard eventually became the vice president of a drug company in Louisville. But he still loves watching basketball—especially college basketball. "Whenever I can, I love to watch, and I love talking to the fans," Beard says.

He sighs. "I just love basketball."

# CHAPTER 2

# FRANK RAMSEY

Frank Ramsey was a notable baseball and basketball player at Madisonville High School, but it took more than that to impress Adolph Rupp. His first meeting with the legendary UK coach was more of a one-way conversation. "They had a cubby-hole-sized office then," Ramsey says. "There were two desks, one for Rupp and one for [assistant coach] Harry Lancaster. But there was a bar over Coach Rupp's door, a 6-foot-2 bar, and I made sure to bump my head when I went in the office so I could show I had height.

"Overall, it was friendly," Ramsey says. "We didn't say much, but I believe I told him I wanted to come to school and play for him. That's how I recruited myself to the school." And Ramsey's initiative paid off. Rupp began to watch the big guard who could dribble and drive to the basket. The coach was sure he would fit in as a Wildcat.

"I went there to go to school," Ramsey says. "I was a student first." But Ramsey was a talented basketball player, and he would find himself in the middle of one of the most trying and successful times in Kentucky basketball history.

## THE SETTING

As a sophomore at UK in 1951, Ramsey was eligible to play in the basketball program. It was a good time to be a Wildcat. Ramsey averaged 10 points a game on a team that defeated Kansas State to win the school's third NCAA Tournament championship—three titles in four seasons. The team, which boasted sophomore Cliff Hagan of Owensboro, center Bill Spivey, and guard Bobby Watson, went 32-2 and undefeated in the SEC.

One year of play for Ramsey and one national title—where could his career go from there? Perhaps Rupp's statement, as noted in Tom Wallace's *University of Kentucky Basketball Encyclopedia,* expresses it best: "If we win by 30, Frank gets three points. If we win by three, he gets 30."

During Ramsey's junior year, the defending national champion Wildcats reloaded as center Lou Tsioropoulos came into the fold. Hagan averaged 21.6 points per game, Ramsey averaged 15.9 points, and Watson averaged 13.1 points. After a 29-3 season and another undefeated run in the SEC, the No. 1 ranked Wildcats were primed, yet again, for a title race. But they were upset in the Eastern Regional finals by tenth-ranked St. John's, 64-57.

\* \* \*

Away from the on-court rivalries, scandal brewed. An independent federal investigation discovered that Wildcats players—including former stars Ralph Beard, Alex Groza, and Bill Spivey—had accepted money to "shave" points during basketball games, changing point spreads to the benefit of gamblers. To this day, Beard insists that although he took $500, he never unfairly altered the outcome of a game. Maybe it should be noted that his record during that time was a robust 130-10, with one NIT championship and two NCAA championships.

Nevertheless, Beard and the other Wildcats involved—who also claimed innocence—were banned from basketball. And Kentucky's team in 1953 was penalized, even though none of the players on that roster were suspected of any wrongdoing. The NCAA ruled that Kentucky could not play basketball for the 1952-53 season.

"So we had to sit out," Ramsey says. "We all decided to just practice all year." Coach Rupp made use of his connections, scheduling a scrimmage game against George Mikan and the Minneapolis Lakers.

---

Frank Ramsey helped lead the Wildcats to their only undefeated season, which was then cut short by an obscure NCAA rule.

"We held our own," Ramsey says. There were also four team scrimmages held in Memorial Coliseum, which were watched by standing-room-only crowds.

"We as a team felt we had not been treated fairly," Ramsey says. Rupp planned to channel the pent-up aggression to the next season. He vowed he would make NCAA officials award him another championship trophy.

* * *

After the 1953 season, Ramsey graduated from UK. He was selected by Boston in the first round of the NBA draft; but instead of playing professionally, Ramsey, Hagan, and Tsioropoulos enrolled in graduate classes at UK and prepared for their third year of Wildcats basketball. Together, they formed the nucleus of a powerhouse basketball team in 1954.

The trio averaged 58 points a game; and with juniors Billy Evans and Gayle Rose in supporting roles, the Wildcats started off well, winning their first seven games by 12 points or more. In the UK Invitational Tournament, the Wildcats defeated No. 13 Duke by 16 and No. 16 LaSalle by 13. They weren't challenged until they met Xavier for the second time that year. But even a spirited effort by the Musketeers ended in a six-point Kentucky victory. It was the closest game the Wildcats would play in the regular season.

The only thing that could slow down this Kentucky team was an intrepid reporter. Louisville *Courier-Journal* reporter Larry Boeck broke the story of the season in January, which revealed an obscure NCAA rule prohibiting graduate students from playing in the NCAA Tournament. Ramsey, Hagan, and Tsioropoulos had lost their last opportunity to play for an NCAA championship. If the Wildcats were invited to the tournament, they would have to go without their three best players.

Kentucky finished the season 24-0, surpassing the 100-point mark six times and winning their 14 SEC games with ease. But due to a scheduling quirk, the Wildcats did not play eighth-ranked LSU. The Bayou Bengals also finished the SEC regular season with a 14-0 record. To determine the SEC champion and the NCAA representative, the conference staged a one-game playoff in Nashville's Memorial Coliseum. Of course, for Kentucky, the stakes were much higher. The Wildcats' undefeated season was on the line.

# THE GAME OF MY LIFE
## NO. 1 KENTUCKY 63, NO. 7 LOUISIANA STATE 56
## MARCH 9, 1954
### BY FRANK RAMSEY

Coach Rupp wasn't in the best of health for that game, I remember that. He had a patch over his eye, and he'd had some chest pains.

I knew this might be the last college game I was going to play in. I just remember we had to win the game, because an undefeated season was something no one else had ever done before.

But I had a lot going on at that time. We had this game, and I was going into the Army soon. My wife was a cheerleader, and we were going to get married. I was going to be playing pro ball soon. But first we had to win that game. We wanted that undefeated season.

The thing is, it's really the only close game we played all season. At the half we were only up a couple of points [32-28], and in the second half, they came out and took the lead on us [40-36]. Now, we hadn't been down in the second half that whole season, so this was something new for us; but we weren't nervous. We were all collegiate veteran players.

We took a timeout, and we came over to the huddle. Coach Lancaster told us to put on the press, so we did. I'd been getting a lot of shots, and when we pressed, we ended up getting a lot of baskets in the transition game. That's how we ended up winning: we sped up the game and it worked.

I had a good game, 30 points, and I felt good I played that well. So we won [63-56], and we kept our undefeated season. But maybe the big decision was after the game. That's when everybody talked about what we wanted to do with the [NCAA Tournament] bid.

We were against it. Hagan and Tsioropoulos and I didn't want to play in the NCAAs because we felt we'd lose our undefeated season. The others wanted to, and there may have been some kind of vote, but I didn't know about it. Afterward Coach Rupp just said no. He told us we would not be going.

### Statline:

| FG | FT | FTA | PTS |
|----|----|-----|-----|
| 13 | 4 | 5 | 30 |

# THE RESULT

"I just remember thinking it was all over," Ramsey says of his college career. "There was no celebration after the LSU game. We all had Cokes, and Coach Rupp said we weren't accepting the NCAA bid. I think some were disappointed that we didn't go on and play. But to me, having the unbeaten season is something that will never be repeated."

And an NCAA victory would have been difficult, he says. "You'd have taken all those points away if we didn't play," Ramsey says. "It would've been very hard."

In his book *Hello Everybody, This is Cawood Ledford*, the legendary UK announcer, who was concluding his rookie year of Wildcats play-by-play at the time, speaks of the aftermath of the LSU game as recounted to him by Frank Ramsey. "As Ramsey later told me, Rupp came back to the locker room," Ledford wrote. "[Rupp] said, 'We're not going [to the tournament] because I'm not going to take a bunch of turds like you to the NCAA.'"

When the NCAA Tournament was over that season, LaSalle, which had lost to Kentucky in the regular season, was crowned champion. "We knew we could've beaten them—we already had beaten them," Ramsey says. "That's when we knew we were the best team in college basketball that year."

* * *

Afterward, Ramsey got married, completed a stint in the Army, and started his professional basketball career—which was more successful than anyone could have imagined. After playing for one of the greatest college coaches in UK history, Ramsey went on to play for legendary Boston Celtics coach Red Auerbach; and over his nine-season career, Ramsey averaged 13.4 points per game.

Ramsey had arrived in Boston in the prime of Auerbach's coaching career, and he was the first to make the role of the sixth man—or the first man coming off the bench in a game—popular in the NBA. As a Celtic, Ramsey was a member of seven world championship teams.

"I learned a tremendous amount from both of them," Ramsey says of Rupp and Auerbach, who passed away in 2006. "I learned about self-discipline and hard work and how it pays off. Both were dictators, but I don't know of any continual winning team that isn't coached by a dictator."

But Ramsey notes a distinct difference in Rupp and Auerbach's coaching styles. "Coach Rupp took a bunch of boys from the hills and said, 'If you fit into my system and do it my way, you'll win.' And he made believers out of you. Coach Auerbach was a great evaluator of talent, and he was more concerned about how the player fit into his team."

# AFTER BLUE

After nine seasons and seven championships, Ramsey retired from playing basketball. He coached the ABA's Kentucky Colonels for one season. The Boston Celtics later retired his number, 23. Ramsey then returned to his hometown of Madisonville, where he and his family still live. Currently, he serves as president of the Dixon Bank.

In 1981, Ramsey was inducted into the basketball Hall of Fame. "What an honor," he says. In 2005, Ramsey's life took another dramatic turn when a tornado destroyed his home, as well as the homes of several other Madisonville residents. Unfortunately, much of his championship memorabilia was swept away. "If I was there at the time, I could've been swept up, too," he says. "In that sense, we were lucky."

When talking about Kentucky basketball, Ramsey says he reflects fondly on that undefeated team. "We were a close bunch," he says. "A lot of us still get together every once and a while to catch up. We were always together, and we all turned out to be very successful. No one can ever take that undefeated season away from us. And I don't think anyone will ever do it again."

# CHAPTER 3

# VERNON HATTON

Since his high school basketball days at Lafayette, Vernon Hatton has excelled at the pressure shot. "You've got to have confidence in yourself," Hatton says. "And you've got to want the ball when it matters. At the end of the game, when there's a difference between winning and losing, you have to know you're going to make the shot."

And Hatton had the confidence. "I always wanted it," he says. "I didn't mind the pressure. I just wanted to be the one to make that shot. Somebody has to shoot at the end, and that's what I liked to do."

After Hatton was honored as a Kentucky all-star player, he was named to the Chuck Taylor All-Star team, which was comprised of merely five players from Kentucky.

As a big, 6-foot-3 guard from Lexington, Hatton seemed right for the University of Kentucky. And naturally, coach Adolph Rupp wanted him on the team. "He was just a big, intimidating coach," Hatton says of Rupp. "He was rough, and he was mean." He pauses. "But he was a good, good coach," he says. "Sometimes it took a player ten years before they realized how good a coach he was."

## THE SETTING

The Wildcats were in the middle of a dynastic period during the mid-1950s. Following national championships in 1946, 1948, 1949, and 1951, along with conference titles in 1951, 1952, 1954, and 1955, many were beginning to realize that Lexington was a special place in the world of college basketball.

Vernon Hatton dove right into the middle of the Big Blue Storm. In 1956, Hatton's sophomore year and UK basketball debut, Kentucky was rebuilding; the team finished with a 20-6 record but lost to Iowa in the second round of the NCAA Tournament. Hatton averaged 13.3 points per game, but the Wildcats were led by 6-foot-7 center Bob Burrow, who averaged 21.1 points, and 6-foot-6 forward Jerry Bird, who averaged 16.2 points. The foundation for the Wildcats' fourth NCAA Championship team was laid in the next season.

A year later, Hatton increased his average to 14.8 points per game; but sensational newcomer Johnny Cox, a 6-foot-4 sophomore forward, consistently scored 19.4 points per contest. Junior center Ed Beck held his own in the paint, while 6-foot-3 forward John Crigler posed another threat, scoring just over 10 points per game.

In that season, the Wildcats finished 23-5 and won the SEC championship, earning a No.3 national ranking. But again, the team lost in the second round of the NCAAs—this time to No.11 Michigan State, 80-68. Nevertheless, with a solid core of returning talent, the Wildcats looked to be a contender again in the 1957-58 season.

Of course, there were some skeptics—including the team's own coach. "They might be pretty good barnyard fiddlers, but we have a Carnegie Hall schedule, and it will take violinists to play that schedule," said Rupp, according to the team's media guide. Rupp said the team was infamous for "fiddlin' around and fiddlin' around and then finally pulling it out at the end." That's how the team became known as The Fiddlin' Five.

\* \* \*

Beck, Hatton, Crigler, and fellow senior Adrian Smith formed a powerful nucleus of senior team-leaders, and high-scoring Cox bolstered the offense. The Wildcats had quickness and experience; and they would need all of it for the schedule that lie ahead.

After opening with close wins over traditional powers Duke (78-74) and Ohio State (61-54), Kentucky faced its toughest test—possibly in the history of the program—from one of the best teams in the country: Temple.

In early December, with a packed house in Memorial Coliseum, Kentucky and Temple were prepared to stage one of the most memorable games in the history of college basketball. Temple entered the contest with All-American Guy Rodgers, a consistent scorer. As long

Vernon Hatton (No. 52) became known for his clutch shots while playing for the Big Blue.

as the Owls maintained a relentless, aggressive offense, they would be dangerous.

Hatton would lead his team in scoring throughout the season, averaging more than 17 points per game. But he would have one of his worst games—in regulation time—against Temple. Until the pressure was on, that is.

# THE GAME OF MY LIFE
### KENTUCKY 85, TEMPLE 83 (3 OT)
### DECEMBER 7, 1957
### BY VERNON HATTON

It's hard to remember back that far, and a lot's been written about that game. But I do know I didn't play that well throughout the game, not until the overtimes, anyway.

I remember that Johnny Cox had a great game, keeping us in it with his scoring [22 points], and I think Adrian Smith did, too [18 points]. That Temple team was a good squad, and we knew they were. I just wasn't having that great of a game, even though for the fans, it was a great game to watch.

I remember Temple got a lead on us [eight points] but once we came back, it was close all the way through until the half [Temple led 35-34]. We seemed to go back and forth all through the second half, too. But everybody always wants to talk about the overtimes.

We were down a point with about 30 seconds to go in regulation, and I was able to hit a free throw to tie it. I never had a problem with having the ball in my hands when the game was close. I wasn't nervous; I wanted to do it.

We did get the ball one last time in regulation, and we had one last shot to win. Coach Rupp told us to get it to Adrian Smith. So we got it to him, and he threw up a long shot but missed. That led to the first overtime.

The Temple team kept playing, and they got a lead [four points]. We came back again. Then, with a few seconds to go in that first overtime, [Rodgers, Temple's All-American,] hit a jumper to put them up by two, and we called a timeout with one second to go.

Coach Rupp said again that we should get the ball to Smith. But this time an assistant coach said, 'Why don't you let Vernon shoot it?' So I looked up, and I said, 'Yeah, why can't I do it?' Coach Rupp thought about it and said to me, 'Well, you haven't done anything else in this game. Give it a try.'

When Crigler threw it in to me, I was about 47, 48 feet away from the basket. I got off a set shot, and it went in as the buzzer went off. Back then, we didn't have three-pointers, so it just counted as a simple two points. I say it all the time, and I still think it: that shot should've been a five-pointer.

In the second overtime, we kept going back and forth. We were up by two [75-73] when one of their players [Mel Brodsky] hit a couple of free throws to force a third overtime. By then we just wanted to finish the thing and get the win. Other than hitting that long shot, I still hadn't done a whole lot in the game. So this was when I started really making a difference.

We were tied again [at 81] when I hit a basket. Then I was fouled, and I hit two free throws. After that, they missed a shot to tie it again, and finally, it was over. That was how we won the longest game in the history of Kentucky basketball.

**Statline:**

| FG | FT | FTA | PTS |
|----|----|-----|-----|
| 5 | 7 | 9 | 17 |

# THE RESULT

"I had a decent game," he says. "I only had 17 points, but I did hit that long shot; and I scored six points in the last five minutes."

The game was made even more famous by the coverage it received in the nation's newspapers. Herb Good, of *The Philadelphia Inquirer,* had followed Temple and reported back to East Coast fans. Good called Hatton's basket "a sensational 47-foot shot as the buzzer ended a five-minute overtime session."

But the game was also marred by tragedy. Good reported that the game was "a super-duper thriller that was filled with such suspense that one of the 12,300 died from the excitement before it was over." It was true. William Baughn, a former Lexington City Commissioner, collapsed from a heart attack with about 30 seconds to go in regulation. He missed the best parts of the game.

After the game, Hatton approached Rupp and did something he'd never done before: he asked for the game ball. "He told me I couldn't have it," Hatton says. "I got so mad, and I started to walk away. And then, of course, he let me have it."

As Kentucky's season continued, Rupp's prediction was proven correct—the team played inconsistently against a challenging schedule. After the Temple victory, the Wildcats lost three of their next four games against Maryland, Southern Methodist, and West Virginia.

Many wondered if the team could right the ship. But not to worry—the Wildcats posted a 15-3 record to finish the season, winning the SEC Championship again and earning a No. 9 national ranking. And then came the Wildcats' ultimate challenge: The NCAA Tournament.

The Fiddlin' Five started off well, defeating unranked Miami, Ohio, 94-70 before a home crowd in Lexington. In the second round, they faced No. 8 Notre Dame. Again, with the home crowd behind them, Kentucky steamrolled the competition, demolishing the Irish 89-56. Finally it seemed as if the Wildcats were living up to their potential.

Next up was a trip to the Final Four—new territory for the players on this Kentucky team. Fortunately for the Wildcats, the tournament was held at Freedom Hall, just down the road in Louisville. Remarkably, the Wildcats remained in their home state for the entirety of their 1958 NCAA Tournament run. But more worries lie ahead. An old nemesis was waiting for Kentucky in the Final Four—one that sought revenge against the Big Blue, and especially Vernon Hatton.

Now ranked fifth in the nation, the Temple Owls had reeled off a stellar season and rode it all the way to the Final Four. When they played Kentucky for the second time that year, the game was eerily similar.

After one half, the score was tied at 31. And, as *Courier-Journal* reporter Larry Boeck went on to describe for his readers, "Vernon Hatton did it to Temple again."

Kentucky led by seven in the first half and five in the second. But Temple rallied back and led by four with under three minutes to play. Then, Temple attempted to stall, holding the ball and watching as the clock ran out. But the Owls' strategy failed. Adrian Smith made three consecutive free throws after being fouled. After Temple missed a shot, Beck got the rebound and called timeout.

The Wildcats were down a point with 16 seconds remaining. A trip to the national championship game against Elgin Baylor and Seattle was hanging in the balance. It was time for Vernon Hatton to take control. This time the play was drawn up for Hatton. He took the inbounds pass at the top of the circle, dribbled right off of a screen by Beck, went down the baseline, and scored a layup for the victory. He accumulated 13 points in the game.

\* \* \*

Knowing that the Seattle matchup would require a Herculean effort, Hatton saved what is perhaps his best game for last. Vernon Hatton scored 30 points, sinking 12 of 15 shots from the free-throw line. Teammates Cox [24 points] and Crigler [14 points] also executed stellar performances. The combined handiwork of Hatton and his fellow Wildcats helped to offset Baylor's 25 points and 19 rebounds.

While Hatton's scoring helped keep Kentucky in the game, the Wildcats trailed by 11 points on two separate occasions. Finally, Seattle grew tired. Kentucky first gained the lead with six minutes to play and then ran away with the Wildcats' fourth—and Adolph Rupp's last—NCAA title. "That proved it," Hatton says. "We thought we could beat anyone, and that proved it."

After the game, Rupp uttered his now famous words. "Those

boys certainly are not concert violinists," he said of his team, "but they sure can fiddle."

# AFTER BLUE

Hatton continued his athletic career in the National Basketball Association, where he played for four seasons with Philadelphia and St. Louis. He averaged 5.5 points per game. Now, Hatton works as a realtor and auctioneer in Lexington, and he is still remembered fondly by Kentucky basketball fans.

In a 2006 poll of the most clutch players in Kentucky basketball history, the winner was not a player from the Pitino or Hall eras. The winner was Vernon Hatton. And after examining the evidence, who could argue?

"I'm proud of that," Hatton says. "I like being known as the player who should take that big shot."

The Fiddlin' Five became known as one of the greatest teams in Kentucky history, due in large part to Vernon Hatton's renowned clutch play. "Confidence," he says, laughing. "That's all you need."

# CHAPTER 4

# COTTON NASH

Charles "Cotton" Nash saw much of the country while he was growing up, but he always knew that basketball was king in Kentucky. His father's job required the family to frequently pack up and relocate; and so, by the time Cotton graduated high school, he had already lived in Indiana, New Jersey, and Louisiana.

Cotton spent the itinerant years of his youth playing basketball and honing his game. Over the course of his high school career, Nash grew to 6-foot-5 and developed the quickness, ball-handling skills, and deadly outside shooting touch to be an elite big guard. However, because of his agility, Nash could also work inside and beat bigger and slower players off the dribble.

As a senior at Lake Charles High School, Nash was named a *Parade* All-American. Basketball powers like Michigan State and UCLA vied for his services. "I was recruited pretty heavy," Nash says. "I made my decision based on what would be the best conference for basketball at the time. So I made my decision to go play in the SEC. Kentucky basketball was legendary," he says. "I was willing to try the best."

## THE SETTING

Although Nash arrived at Kentucky with a reputation as a talented baseball player too, his destiny lay on the basketball court. Kentucky basketball had become synonymous with excellence, but the landscape was changing. By the early 1960s, much of the college basketball world's focus had shifted to Ohio, where Ohio State and Cincinnati were winning national championships. The decade would also mark the inception of John Wooden's dynasty at UCLA.

Kentucky was no longer getting its choice of the nation's greatest players. For three seasons, Nash would carry the team single-handedly. If he did not bear the burden, it would have been "lean years at UK," as legendary Kentucky radio broadcaster Cawood Ledford stated in his autobiography, *Hello Everybody, This is Cawood Ledford*.

During Nash's first year on the varsity basketball squad, he played as an undersized center; but he still led the team with 23.4 points per game. Along with senior guard Larry Pursiful and junior guard Scotty Baesler, the Wildcats laid down a record of 23-3, won a share of the SEC Championship, and earned a No. 3 national ranking. The only thing that stood between the Wildcats and a possible national title was a 10-point loss to No. 1 Ohio State.

But Rupp may have done more harm than good with his aggressive coaching style, according to Ledford. Few Kentucky basketball players had Nash's combination of charisma, good looks, and outright talent. But sometimes his brashness and shot selection were at odds with head coach Adolph Rupp. Ledford wrote that assistant coach Harry Lancaster and Adolph Rupp criticized Nash after the Wildcats' loss to Ohio State.

"He [Lancaster] and Coach Rupp read Cotton the riot act," Ledford wrote, "telling [Nash] he was a gutless player who couldn't produce against the good teams. It might have ruined him," Ledford recalled.

But Nash was one of Ledford's favorites. "I've never understood why Cotton Nash took so many knocks," Ledford wrote. "As far as I'm concerned, they ought to build a monument to the guy. After UK had gone 19-9 in 1960-61, he absolutely carried the program on his back for the next three years."

\* \* \*

The Wildcats struggled during Cotton's junior year, largely because the team depended exclusively upon Nash to sink the shots. Cotton averaged more than 20 points per game for the 16-9 squad.

Help arrived the following season in the form of an outstanding sophomore class. From Ashland, 6-foot-3 forward Larry Conley averaged 12-plus points per game. Tommy Kron and Mickey Gibson became viable backups. Junior Terry Mobley and senior Ted Deeken

Cotton Nash kept the Kentucky tradition alive—almost single-handedly—in the 1960s.

stepped up their game to diversify the Wildcats' previously limited scoring options.

Finally, Nash had some assistance on the court. But the Wildcats still lacked height, and even though many agreed Nash would be best utilized as a big guard, he was forced to again play center. During Nash's senior year, the Wildcats began the season 9-0 and reached No. 2 in the rankings. However, they had not faced a ranked team in that stretch of victories.

Their tenth game, the Sugar Bowl Classic championship in New Orleans, would be different. Ninth-ranked Duke, which sported a huge front line, awaited Kentucky. The Blue Devils also featured All-American Jeff Mullins, a 6-foot-4 scorer from Lexington Lafayette High School, and Kentucky's Mr. Basketball in 1960.

Those who questioned Nash's ability to step up his play in the big games would think differently after this contest.

# THE GAME OF MY LIFE
## NO. 2 KENTUCKY 81, NO. 8 DUKE 79
### DECEMBER 31, 1963
#### BY COTTON NASH

It was New Year's Eve, 1963. We'd started the season 9-0, and we knew that if we won this game we'd be No. 1 in the polls the next week. We had a front line of me—a 6-foot-5 center—and two 6-foot-3 forwards. We were actually smaller than Rupp's Runts, and we were going up against Duke, which had a frontline measuring at 7 feet, 6-foot-11, and 6-foot-8.

It was a nip-and-tuck game the whole way. We played them close because we were outrunning them the whole game. Their guards were 6-foot-5, which was as big as me, so we had to utilize our quickness. We had to push against them, tire them out, and just keep running. But they were real, real good.

At the half, we were down [47-37] but we knew that the game was still close enough to make a run. I'd been able to use my speed to get around my man, and that's how I was scoring; so we kept doing it, and I had about 20 points in the second half.

I remember Mobley hadn't done very much in our previous game [he actually scored one point in an 86-64 win over Loyola of Louisiana], and up to a point, he hadn't done much in our game with Duke either. But we were down two points with [27 seconds] to go, and he hit one from the corner to tie it. That was a big shot.

So when [Ted Deeken] batted the ball out of one of their players' hands, it went right to Kron, and he got it and called timeout. I think everyone thought the ball would be coming to me. I did, too—that was the play we called. But the defense really kept me covered.

So Randy Embry dribbled out most of the clock before he found Mobley open, and he fired it to him and Mobley put up a [13-foot] shot and banked it in. He had to hit the big shot, so he did. And that Sugar Bowl championship was the thing we were probably most proud of.

When the polls came out the next week, we were No. 1 again for the first time since 1958. We resurrected the program.

**Statline:**

| FG | FGA | FT | FTA | REB | PTS |
|----|-----|----|----|-----|-----|
| 13 | 29  | 4  | 8  | 5   | 30  |

# THE RESULT

"Mobley may have been the last Wildcat the Blue Devils expected to take the vital shot," *The Courier-Journal* reported after the game. "Nash held the hot hand with his 30 points, and Deeken, who came to life in the second half, had 18 points."

Mobley, a native of Harrodsburg, averaged 13.4 points on the season, but posted just five points before his two big shots to tie and win the game. After the winning shot, Rupp raced onto the court and grabbed Mobley.

"Coach Rupp never came out onto the court to congratulate us after a win," Mobley told Lexington broadcaster Denny Trease. "But this time I noticed him hurrying straight toward me. He said, 'Remember, Harrodsburg [Mobley], we knew Duke was expecting Nash to get the ball, so we outsmarted them and instructed you to take the last shot.'"

The next day, Mobley saw the headline in the New Orleans newspaper. "Rupp surprises Duke," it read. "Calls on Mobley to take the winning shot."

\* \* \*

Nash scored 58 points in the games against Loyola and Duke and was named MVP of the Sugar Bowl Classic. Mullins, the Kentucky native, finished with 26 points but could not produce a victory.

Unfortunately, Nash's Wildcats were a mix of youth and inconsistency during his senior season. After reaching No. 1 in the country, UK won the SEC championship; but the Wildcats averaged only 53 points in the three games immediately preceding the NCAA Tournament. The offense vanished—except for Nash—but still, UK was 21-4 and No. 4 in the nation.

Just one day before their first-round NCAA Tournament game, the Wildcats faced another problem. Gibson, a 6-foot-2 guard and valuable rebounder, was kicked off the team for disciplinary reasons. It was a tough blow to a team that already had rebounding difficulties.

Inconsistent and unable to score enough to compensate for their lack of height, the Wildcats lost to unranked Ohio University 85-69 in the first round of the NCAA Tournament. Nash scored just 10 points. He scored 23 points in the consolation game, a 100-91 loss to eighth-ranked Loyola of Chicago. His career was over, and he would never taste a Final Four or a national championship.

Nevertheless, without Nash's talent, the Kentucky program never would have returned to crack the top ten in the polls. When he left Kentucky, he had scored 1,770 points. Nash averaged 24 points and 11.7 rebounds as a senior, becoming the only UK player to average more than 20 points over three consecutive seasons. His 22.7 career scoring average is second only to Dan Issel's 25.8.

# AFTER BLUE

"We had resurrected the program by that senior year," Nash says. "That was a great feeling." After leaving Kentucky, Nash was drafted No. 14 overall in the second round of the 1964 NBA Draft by the Los Angeles Lakers. He played for one season, averaging three points per game, before he tried his hand at Major League Baseball. Over three seasons, he saw limited action as a first baseman and outfielder with the Chicago White Sox and the Minnesota Twins. Then he returned to professional basketball, playing a season with the ABA's Kentucky Colonels and averaging 8.5 points per game. After retiring from both leagues, Nash returned to Lexington where he established a real estate and investment company.

And all these years later, Nash says he holds Coach Rupp in great esteem. "I enjoyed playing for him," he says. "We got in at 3:15 every day and we got out at 5 p.m. Everything was in motion and there was never a wasted minute. He was good that way about practices. For some, it took a long time to grow to like Coach Rupp."

But more than anything, Nash looks fondly on his place in Kentucky history. "It makes me proud to say I helped keep the tradition going," he says. "To beat Duke, that was definitely our biggest game."

# CHAPTER 5

# LOUIE DAMPIER

Few athletes in the history of Kentucky basketball were better shooters than Louie Dampier; and few teams—if any—in the school's history were more beloved than Rupp's Runts, the 1965-66 National Runners-up. The unheralded squad, nicknamed for its collective lack of height, was picked in the preseason to finish third in the SEC; and the Runts opened with 23 consecutive victories before making a run to the national title game against previously underestimated Texas Western.

The fans' love for the team was never more apparent than on the 40-year Runts reunion in 2006, when members of the squad were honored at Rupp Arena before a basketball game. Thousands of fans arrived before the game to have members of the team sign posters, T-shirts, and pictures.

"It's unbelievable—that's the only word I can think of," says Dampier, an All-American from Indianapolis. "We came back here, it's 40 years later, and we got *beat* in the national championship. It's not like we're one of the best teams to ever play here. Only in Kentucky. The fans here are absolutely unbelievable."

It's something Dampier says players won't even realize until years later. "I tried to tell the [2005-06 team] in the locker room today, 'You're going through this now, and you think you know all there is to know about this, but you don't have a clue,'" he says. "I don't think it really dawned on me until I'd been out."

* * *

They called him Little Louie. As a student at Southport High

31

School, Dampier carved his legend, scoring 673 points his senior year—more than any other Indiana prep player. Averaging 24 points per game, the 6-foot guard became known for the perfect form on his jumper and the long range on his shot. He was an all-around athlete who would also play baseball at UK. And he served as Southport's class president for two years.

Dampier was a leader who could shoot—an ideal candidate for coach Adolph Rupp's team.

# THE SETTING

Louie Dampier and his starting lineup teammates—6-foot-5 guard Tommy Kron, 6-foot-5 center Thad Jaracz, and 6-foot-4 forwards Larry Conley and Pat Riley—are always thought of as 'The Team that Lost to Texas Western.' After the release of the 2006 Disney movie *Glory Road,* which depicted the 1966 national title game in which an all-white UK starting five faced the all-black starters from Texas Western, the epithet stuck for a whole new generation.

Kentucky was the super-talented team—the team that could not be beaten. It was mistakenly assumed by many that Texas Western had no chance. But Texas Western was ranked No. 3 in the country and featured a cat-quick backcourt on an overall talented team.

Despite the hype surrounding the Runts' championship game loss to Texas Western, there were many other memorable moments during the 1965-66 season. For Dampier, that moment was February 2, 1966, the day he scored a career-high 42 points in the biggest game of the year up to that point.

\* \* \*

The prospects for the 1965-66 season did not look good. The Kentucky Wildcats were coming off a 15-10 campaign the previous season, which ended without an invitation to the NCAA or NIT tournaments, and they were excluded from the preseason polls. They were not even thought to figure in the conference race.

Oh, how the so-called experts were wrong. A new assistant basketball

---

"Little" Louie Dampier was a member of Rupp's Runts, one of the most beloved teams in Kentucky basketball history.

coach, with a new training regimen, invaded Kentucky's campus. The athletes on the team would run like they'd never run before.

"We had a new assistant coach, by the name of Joe B. Hall," Conley said in an interview with the University of Kentucky. "We ran. And I left some green beans and mashed potatoes out there, I tell ya."

Kentucky had always been known for running and scoring baskets in transition. But this team would surpass historical precedent. Conley and others credited Hall's training program with improving the team's athleticism—and it showed on the court.

The team featured no starter taller than 6-foot-5. Surely, coach Adolph Rupp could not coax a champion out of a group with such a lack of height. But although the team was small at the forward and center positions, the Runts also boasted Kron, the versatile 6-foot-5 guard.

With deadly shooting and quickness, the Runts raced out to a 15-0 record and a No. 2 national ranking, winning at Illinois and Virginia. They crushed Indiana by 35, Notre Dame by 34.

Third-ranked Vanderbilt posed the first threat to the Wildcats' NCAA Tournament aspirations. But the Runts defeated Vandy 96-83. Riley and Dampier carried the team in scoring during the winning streak. However, Kentucky would later have to travel to the Commodores' dangerous arena in Nashville for a rematch to secure the SEC championship and the automatic berth into the NCAA Tournament.

The rematch was bizarrely similar to the original contest—Kentucky was ranked No. 2, and again, Vanderbilt was ranked No. 3. The SEC title was on the line, and Louie Dampier stepped up his game. "Louie got 42 points that day," Kron says during the press conference of the 40-year Runts reunion. "He absolutely shot the lights out."

"Oh—was it 42?" Dampier laughs.

Yes, it was. Forty-two points. A career-high.

# THE GAME OF MY LIFE
## NO. 2 KENTUCKY 105, NO. 3 VANDERBILT 90
### FEBRUARY 2, 1966
#### BY LOUIE DAMPIER

That year, we went to Vanderbilt, and back then you had to win your conference championship to get into the [NCAA] Tournament. Leading up to the big game, which was the NCAA final, that Vandy game was very important to us that year.

I have a poor memory about reflecting on games, but I remember a few things about that one. I know going into it we had time to prepare, and we knew that Vandy team well. But we prepared for it just like it was any other game. Coach Rupp had a way of telling us that every game was important, so we didn't really put any added importance on it.

They were a good team—they had more height than we did, like most of the teams that year. But we did what we did all season: we pushed the ball on them and took good shots. We were quick, but they ran the same kind of offense. They wanted to push the ball up the court, too, which is why it was such a high-scoring game, 105-90. There was no shot clock then, but that didn't matter to either of our teams.

In games like that, when you're making shots, you feel good. I felt good in that game. I knew it when I put up a shot that bounced high off the rim and fell through. I knew then I was feeling good.

I also knew I was having a pretty good game when the Vandy players starting getting physical with me. They'd push me; they knocked me down a few times. And then Riley came over and said, 'Enough of that' to them. I don't know if that had any effect or not. But you know you're doing good when the other team tries to get to you. They weren't trying to hurt me, but they wanted to get to me mentally. I got a couple of three-point plays because of those fouls.

After the game, Coach Rupp gave us his post-game talk, and they were usually pretty short. Then Riley looked at a stat sheet, and he just said, '42 points!' We didn't know I had that many. I knew I had a lot, but not that many.

**Statline:**

| FG | FGA | FT | FTA | REB | PF | PTS |
|---|---|---|---|---|---|---|
| 18 | 29 | 6 | 6 | 9 | 2 | 42 |

# THE RESULT

Rupp's Runts continued to dazzle for the rest of the season, racking up a 27-2 record, 15-1 in the SEC. They ended the season ranked No. 1 in the nation. They defeated Dayton in a tough 86-79 contest in the NCAA first round before beating ninth-ranked Michigan 84-77. And in the Final Four, the Wildcats bested second-ranked Duke 83-79 in what many thought was the real championship game—a prelude to an easy win in the title contest.

But Texas Western thought differently. The Miners held the

Wildcats to a season-low 38.6 percent shooting from the field and outrebounded them 35-33. Trailing 7-3 early, Miners guard Bobby Joe Hill stole two passes and converted them into layups on the other end. Texas Western took a 13-8 lead and never looked back, ending one of the most magical seasons UK fans had ever seen.

"They were probably the biggest surprise of any team I followed," legendary UK radio broadcaster Cawood Ledford said of the Runts team in an interview with the university.

# AFTER BLUE

Dampier has long been one of the most popular Wildcats in the history of the Kentucky program. He scored 18 points in his first college game and led the 1964-65 team in scoring with 17 points per game. During the Rupp's Runts season, he shot 51.6 percent from the field; and if the three-point shot was available, his scoring average of 21.1 would surely have been more. He scored 23 points in Kentucky's win over Duke in the 1966 Final Four and 19 points in the championship loss to Texas Western. During his junior and senior seasons, he earned All-America honors.

Dampier completed his college career with a cumulative 1,575 points. But that was just the beginning. Dampier was brilliant in professional basketball, becoming the all-time leading scorer in the history of the American Basketball Association. He led the Kentucky Colonels to a championship and finished with 13,725 points.

After several years in private business, Dampier and Dan Issel, another former Wildcat, teamed up as assistant coaches with the NBA's Denver Nuggets. After retiring from business and basketball, he settled in Oldham County outside Louisville.

"Everyone always focuses on the Texas Western game," says Kron. "But that Vanderbilt game was really a big one. And they were all big in the tournament. And that defining moment in the title game was, unfortunately, a loss. But we don't like to dwell on that."

"I've had a great time getting back together with the guys, reminiscing," Dampier says of the Runts' reunion. "The word 'remember' came up a lot. 'Remember this, remember that.' We started out underrated, and through the season we put a string of wins together.

"We ended up No. 1. It's good to remember."

# CHAPTER 6

# DAN ISSEL

According to a local newspaper, Dan Issel wasn't among the Wildcats' recruiting targets for 1966. But that didn't stop Joe B. Hall from seeking out the talented 6-foot-8 Parade All-American.

"Issel was a player with great potential, and we didn't want to let him get away," Joe B. Hall, Kentucky's main recruiter at the time, told Denny Trease in the book *Tales From the Kentucky Hardwood.*

After losing most of the Rupp's Runts national runners-up team, the Wildcats were looking for size—and Issel filled the bill. Besides sporting a host of low post moves, including a deadly hook shot, Issel could easily move up and down the court—a must in coach Adolph Rupp's fast-paced offense.

## THE SETTING

Issel made his debut as a sophomore, averaging 16 points per game and closely trailing fellow sophomore Mike Casey's impressive 20-point average. Issel contributed 12 rebounds per contest. He erupted for a 36-point, 13-rebound game against Marquette in the first round of the NCAA Tournament. That season, the Wildcats went 22-5, won the SEC, and finished fourth in the national polls. But Kentucky was upset by unranked Ohio State, 82-81, in the NCAA's second round.

As a junior, Issel dominated the court, averaging 26.6 points and 13.6 rebounds per game. He scored 41 points in a game against Vanderbilt and posted 36 points and 29 rebounds against LSU. But after going 23-5 and capturing another SEC title, the Wildcats were upset by Marquette in the first round of the NCAA Tournament, 81-74.

By that time, Issel had blossomed into an All-American. "By playing for Coach Rupp, I was able to develop into a much more complete player," Issel says. "I became a very good shooter. Each day at the start of practice, Coach Rupp would begin with 30 minutes of shooting. That really helped me."

Many UK basketball historians say the Wildcats were a lock for another national championship prior to the 1969-70 season. Issel was returning for his senior season, as was Mike Casey, who balanced the Kentucky offensive attack. But tragedy struck when Casey was involved in a serious car accident that sidelined him for the entire season.

"That really hurt us," Issel says. "Well," Rupp was quoted as saying after hearing the news, "there goes the national championship."

Issel assumed more of the scoring load, upping his average to 33.9 points per game. The Wildcats posted a record of 16-1, losing only to Vanderbilt. But because of the loss, a conference championship was in doubt.

"We hadn't wrapped up the championship yet," Issel says. "So this became a really big game."

But he's too modest. By the 18th game of season, Issel's incredible scoring had put him within reach of a seemingly unattainable goal: overtaking Cotton Nash's career scoring record of 1,770 points. I knew I was getting close," Issel says. "I think I had to have another 40-point game to break the record."

# THE GAME OF MY LIFE
## NO. 3 KENTUCKY 120, MISSISSIPPI 85
### FEBRUARY 7, 1970
#### BY DAN ISSEL

It was not a close game. I didn't realize how many points I was scoring, but I knew if I had a big game, I could get that career scor-

---

Dan Issel still holds 28 individual records, but his Kentucky teams never reached the Final Four.

ing record. Early on, I knew I was having a good game because I wasn't missing many shots. It seemed like everything was going in.

At the half, we were up by a lot of points [56-28], and normally in those kinds of games, other guys would get in and play some. I thought that was probably going to happen. I didn't know how many points I had or where I stood in any of those statistical categories.

So Coach Rupp took me out of the game when there was still maybe a quarter of the game to go. Then, our manager, Doug Billips, told Coach that I had the chance to set the single-game scoring record, which Cliff Hagan had set against Temple in 1953. Hagan scored 51 points in that game.

Now, for some history here: There was an incident during my junior year when the players were revolting against Joe B. Hall's rigorous running program. A lot of the seniors were revolting against it, and they wanted me to talk to Coach Rupp about making it easier. We talked, and Coach Rupp said that if I ran, he would do what he could to get me the single-game record. I ran.

Coach Rupp put me back in the game. I don't remember how many games we had left in the season, but I knew I had the chance to break the career scoring record, which was a marvelous record considering how many great players had gone to Kentucky. But I also knew I could break the single-game mark, which was a huge accomplishment as well.

I remember during the game, there was a close call that could've been a block or a foul that would've been my fifth, and that was before I'd set the single-game record. I took the ball to the hoop, and the officials called it a block, not a charge. I was able to go and knock down two more free throws, which added to my total. That was big.

Still, I didn't know how many points I had until they announced it over the speakers. That's when I heard I'd gotten 53 points. That was it. I had the record.

Coach Rupp didn't say anything to me until after the game. He congratulated me, and he said he was a little sorry to see Cliff's record be broken, but that if he didn't want me to do it, he wouldn't have put me back in.

Of course that wasn't the only record broken that night. My 53 points also broke Cotton Nash's career scoring mark. In one game, I got the two most important scoring records at Kentucky.

But the most significant thing was that my dad was there. My dad and mom only missed three home games while I was on the varsity team. My dad would pick three away games a season so he could come and watch us play on the road. That way, he could visit all the SEC cities. He saved Oxford and Starkville for my senior year. Afterward, I spent time with my dad, and that was really nice.

Even though it was at Ole Miss, they gave me the game ball. And that was 36 years ago, but I still have the ball in my office. People look at it and wonder why it says Ole Miss on it.

### Statline:

| FG | FGA | FT | FTA | REB | PTS |
|----|-----|----|-----|-----|-----|
| 23 | 34 | 7 | 7 | 19 | 53 |

# THE RESULT

The Wildcats won the Mississippi game 120-85. They were led by Issel's 53-point, 19-rebound performance. Later in the year, Issel again broke the 50-point mark in a duel with LSU's scoring machine, "Pistol" Pete Maravich. Pete scored 63, Issel scored 51, and UK won a nationally televised game, 121-105.

"Pete was such a clever player," Issel says. "He wasn't a great shooter, but he was creative with the ball and how he got his points."

Issel continued to add his impressive individual totals. But despite a 26-2 record, another SEC title, and a No. 1 ranking, Issel's spectacular career would end without a trip to the Final Four. The Wildcats were upset in the second round of the NCAA Tournament by Artis Gilmore's Jacksonville squad, 106-100. Issel scored 28 points and grabbed 10 rebounds. Gilmore scored 24 points and pulled down 20 rebounds.

"We had a couple of very good opportunities," he said. "We just couldn't get it done. Coach Rupp was two years from the end of his career, and I wish we could've gotten him back to another Final Four."

# AFTER BLUE

After his time at UK, Issel played professional basketball. As a member of the Kentucky Colonels, he took the court alongside fellow Kentucky alum Louie Dampier and, ironically, nemesis Artis Gilmore. Issel would finally realize his championship dreams when the Colonels won the ABA title in 1975.

"That's why I don't sit and sulk," Issel says. "If I had not won a championship, I would've had some regrets."

Issel became the career-leading scorer in six seasons in the ABA, with 12,823 points. He then played for the NBA's Denver Nuggets for nine seasons. Combined, he scored more than 25,000 points.

But who would he compare himself to in today's game? "There are a couple of centers in the league who can shoot the ball pretty well, like Pau Gasol," he says. "That was like me, able to play in a wide-open style."

Issel served as general manager and also coached the Denver Nuggets for seven seasons in two stints between 1992 and 2001. But he will always be remembered in Kentucky for his incredible scoring. Will anyone ever break his career mark of 2,138 points?

"It's possible. You can play four years now, and there's a three-point line," he says. "But if someone got close, they would leave to go to the NBA. I guess somebody may eventually do it, though.

"I thought Kenny [Walker] had a real good chance to break it," he says. "I tried to talk Rex Chapman into it. I'm a Kentucky fan, so I wanted him to stay for four years and break it. I guess I'm meant to have it a little while longer."

But Issel is convinced that no one will shatter his senior-year scoring mark. "I don't think so—34 points per game is a lot," he says. By the completion his Kentucky basketball career, Issel held 28 individual school records. "For the 25 years of basketball I was a part of," he says, "I just have to thank God for all of it."

# CHAPTER 7

# MIKE FLYNN

Mike Flynn had an amazing high school career at Jeffersonville High. He was the school's all-time leading scorer, the state's Mr. Basketball, and a Parade All-American. The college coaches were knocking at his door, and Flynn had a difficult choice to make.

It came down to Indiana and Kentucky. On the one hand, head coach Bobby Knight was trying to build a contender out of Flynn's home-state Hoosiers. On the other hand, Joe Hall was attempting to carry on the legacy of Adolph Rupp at UK.

"People didn't realize that the Indiana program was down when I was coming out of high school," Flynn says. "Kentucky was on the rise." Flynn was eager to put an end to the recruiting process. He committed to Kentucky.

Once Flynn's decision became public, he received one last phone call from Bobby Knight. "He called me up and said he wanted to talk," Flynn says of Knight. "I told him I was finished with the whole recruiting process, and he said I'd made a great choice. He said, 'Best of luck,' and that was it. If I had talked with him, he may have talked me out of it," he says. "I just don't know."

But Knight never called again. Indiana's Mr. Basketball was going to Kentucky.

## THE SETTING

For five consecutive games, it looked as if Flynn had made the wrong decision. In his freshman season, No. 7 Kentucky lost a 90-89

43

double-overtime heartbreaker to the unranked Hoosiers in Lexington.

In the 1972-73 season, Flynn watched as unranked Indiana defeated his No. 8 Wildcats 64-58 in Bloomington. When the two teams were matched up later in the NCAA's Mideast Regional, Indiana, which climbed the rankings to No. 6 in the country, again beat Kentucky, 72-65. The Hoosiers advanced to the Final Four. "Everyone back in Indiana was telling me I made the wrong choice," Flynn says. "They told me, 'You should've gone to IU.'"

As a sophomore, Flynn averaged nine points per game for the talented Kentucky squad. The following season, Flynn averaged 11 points for a 13-13 team in the process of rebuilding. Among the losses was a 77-68 defeat to the third-ranked Indiana Hoosiers. "We really wanted to beat Indiana so bad," Flynn says.

Between talented seniors Kevin Grevey, Jimmy Dan Conner, Bob Guyette, and Mike Flynn and newcomers Rick Robey and Jack Givens, the Wildcats felt optimistic about their chances in the 1974-75 season.

Their hopes were demolished during the third game, when No. 15 Kentucky lost to No. 3 Indiana in Bloomington, 98-74. It was yet another defeat at the hands of the Hoosiers; but this loss was worse, according to Flynn. "It all started with them kicking our ass in Bloomington," he says. "Rick Robey got manhandled by Kent Benson. Knight and Coach Hall were yelling, and Knight slapped him upside the head. I thought they were going to go at it. There was bad blood there."

As the season progressed, the Hoosiers raced to a 31-0 record, winning the Big Ten while Kentucky seethed—and got better. The Wildcats entered the NCAA Tournament with a 22-4 record and the SEC title. "We definitely got better as the season went on," Flynn says. "And Coach Hall told us that he would love to play IU again."

In the Mideast Regional Final in Dayton, Ohio, No. 5 Kentucky faced No. 1 Indiana for a spot in the Final Four. "We knew we were going to have to be as physical as them to win," Flynn says. "The day before the game, there were no fouls called at our practice. Everyone was just knocking people down. The next day, everyone was mentally ready for that game."

---

Mike Flynn spurned his hometown Indiana Hoosiers for the Kentucky Wildcats, and helped defeat IU to reach the Final Four.

# THE GAME OF MY LIFE
## NCAA MIDEAST REGIONAL FINAL:
## NO. 5 KENTUCKY 92, NO. 1 INDIANA 90
## MARCH 22, 1975
### BY MIKE FLYNN

I always felt we had a chance to beat them. They were a great team, but we were good, too. On the blackboard before the game, Coach Hall wrote that we would have a celebration at Memorial Coliseum when we returned after the victory.

Before we went out to play, the coaches told Jimmy Dan Conner and me to move the ball up the court and take our shots. They'd never done that before. Our coaches said Indiana was the best when they set up their defense, so we couldn't let them do that. Luckily, Jimmy Dan and I started hitting.

The atmosphere was amazing: the fans were half IU and half UK. On the court, there wasn't a lot of talking, even though it was so emotional. Back then, it was more of a physical game, not a lot of talking. And of course, that was Bob Knight's style—physical. He was a bully, and he wanted his players to be bullies.

It was just nip and tuck in the first half. I always thought Quinn Buckner was overrated. He couldn't shoot. He guarded me in that game, and I felt like I had something to prove. That's what I was thinking.

Both teams were scoring, and it was physical. Guys were getting knocked down. At halftime, we were tied [at 44]. Coach Hall told us to keep playing hard, and that if we did, we would win. We wanted to keep them running, and we needed our guards to keep shooting.

In the second half, I had Buckner on the baseline, and I took a Michael Jordan-type fadeaway. I hit that shot on him, and I knew; I felt I was in the zone, and I could have a big game.

We were playing so well we got a 10-point lead in the second half. But then they started to come back on us. They were matching us. Hell, if we'd played another minute or two, they may have won, because they were really coming back. Everything was so physical throughout the whole game. But they didn't come back. We held on and ended up winning it by two.

It's the greatest basketball game I've ever played in. The celebration was just jubilant. We cut down the nets. I cut down the last strand of the net—and I still have it. I feel kind of bad about it now, but when I cut my strand I shook it at the IU fans. That just felt so good.

I just had one of those great games, because it meant more to me, I guess, being from Indiana. I had never beaten them before.

**Statline:**

| MIN | FG | FGA | A | PTS |
|---|---|---|---|---|
| 38 | 9 | 13 | 5 | 22 |

# THE RESULT

Flynn finally had his victory over Indiana—and he was the catalyst, scoring a team-high 22 points. Grevey and Conner scored 17 points, while Robey and Phillips had 10 points. Givens chipped in eight points.

Benson executed another super-human effort for Indiana, scoring 33 points and grabbing 23 rebounds. Steve Green scored 21 points, while Buckner had eight points, and Bob Wilkerson notched 14 points and 11 rebounds. Scott May played seven minutes after breaking his left wrist a month earlier. He scored just two points.

"The biggest, strongest warriors beat out the normally quicker, more composed men of Bloomington, Ind.," said Gordon S. White of *The New York Times*. Kentucky "shocked Indiana's once mighty defense with agility that disrupted the Hoosiers." Kentucky forced Indiana into 20 turnovers and Wildcats guards Flynn and Conner outscored Indiana's duo of Buckner and Wilkerson 39-22.

On the road home, Kentuckians greeted their team, lining the Interstate and decorating overpasses with congratulatory signs. "That was so wonderful to see," Flynn says. And afterward, just like Coach Hall promised, there was a celebration at Memorial Coliseum.

Kentucky's dream would end in the national title game a week later. After dispatching Syracuse in the national semifinal 95-79, Kentucky faced UCLA for the national championship.

But many Kentucky players felt they lost the game the day before, when UCLA's coach John Wooden announced he would retire following the national title contest. "What pissed me off so much was when Wooden announced his retirement," Flynn says. "They were so motivated. They played real good." The Bruins beat Kentucky to win their tenth championship, 92-85. Flynn scored 10 points in his final UK game.

# AFTER BLUE

After college, Flynn was selected No. 113 by Philadelphia in the seventh round of the 1975 NBA Draft. He was also chosen by Indianapolis in the sixth round of the ABA Draft. Flynn signed on to play for the Pacers. For three seasons he played in Indiana, averaging 6.2 points per game. He then left for Europe, where he won three Swedish championships and led his team in scoring with 25 points per game.

In 2002, Mike Douchant of The Sports Xchange rated the greatest NCAA Tournament games for *USA Today*. Kentucky's victory over Indiana in 1975 ranked No. 8 on the list. (No. 1 was Duke's win over Kentucky in 1992).

"I thought beating Indiana was our national championship," says Flynn, who resides in Jeffersonville with his family. He now runs a company that brokers mortgages.

"People still talk to me about that game," he says. "When we beat Indiana in that game, no one else could tell me I made the wrong choice."

# CHAPTER 8

# KEVIN GREVEY

In high school, Kevin Grevey never set the bar too high. First, the left-handed scorer wanted to start for the team at Taft High School. Then he considered playing college basketball.

"I went to see the old Cincinnati Royals play when I was growing up," he says. "I saw Oscar Robertson and Jerry Lucas and Adrian Smith. Never did I think about playing on that level." But when he developed into the best player in the state of Ohio, Grevey was getting attention from every major collegiate program in the country. Suddenly, he could play college basketball wherever he wanted.

As it turns out, Grevey's basketball career would lead him just down Interstate 75 to Lexington, Kentucky.

"I was in awe of the UK program," Grevey says. "The players, the spirit, and the tradition. All of it. Growing up in Hamilton I was in a cocoon, and after seeing the big Kentucky program, my Mom, my Dad, and my high school coach all said I should go to UK. I knew that's where I was headed."

But Grevey harbored a few doubts. "I was a bit of a difficult recruit, not because I didn't want to play there, but because I needed to prove to myself that I could play there," he says.

## THE SETTING

Grevey joined the Kentucky program as Adolph Rupp's career was winding down. By the time Grevey was a sophomore, assistant coach Joe B. Hall had accepted the unenviable task of succeeding the coaching legend.

Hall was fortunate to have Kevin Grevey on his squad. Few recruits have had as great of an impact on a program in their first varsity season as Grevey. As freshmen, Grevey and the other recruits, labeled the "Super Kittens," went 22-0. Kevin Grevey, Mike Flynn, Jimmy Dan Conner, and Bob Guyette were a close-knit bunch gifted with speed, athleticism, and smarts. As sophomores, the group would have the opportunity to prove how talented they really were.

But the season did not start well. The Super Kittens lost three of their first four games, largely due to their inconsistency. Hall revoked Grevey's starting spot for a brief period and was harshly criticized by fans who claimed he was not the right man to replace Rupp.

In the UK Invitational Tournament, Grevey found his stroke, and the team went on to start the SEC season 5-4. Then they won their next nine games to capture the SEC championship.

A major reason for the turnaround was Kevin Grevey, who scored more than 200 points in the Wildcats final seven games. "I was hitting every shot when I had a clean look," Grevey says. "In one month I doubled my scoring average from nine points to 18."

In the last two SEC games, Kentucky defeated Auburn 91-79 and Tennessee 86-81 to seize the title. Grevey scored 62 points in the victories. "That Tennessee game was a huge game for me personally," Grevey says. "There I really established myself as a scorer and probably clinched the Player of the Year Award."

But he humbly attributes his offensive success to teamwork. "You can't come off those picks unless someone sets the picks for you," Grevey says. "And my sophomore season, I was voted the best player in the league, but [6-foot-11 center] Jim Andrews was the best player on our team."

After securing the SEC Championship and the NCAA Tournament bid, the Wildcats lost to Indiana 72-65 in the NCAA second round, finishing the year with a record of 20-8. Grevey averaged more than 18 points per game. Aside from Andrews, the majority of the team was returning, and the next season seemed to promise great things.

But the loss of Andrews proved too difficult for the squad to overcome. Kentucky lacked a dominant big man on the inside, and the

---

Kevin Grevey felt John Wooden's retirement announcement ruined his chance at a national title.

Wildcats suffered a 13-13 campaign. Grevey averaged upwards of 21 points per game, but the team needed help. Fans began to boo in Memorial Coliseum—the season couldn't end soon enough.

During the summer, Hall took the Wildcats on a 19-game exhibition tour. The team posted a record of 17-2 and restored some lost confidence. And they would need it. The next year the Wildcats would be talented, but they would also be tested.

\* \* \*

In 1974, Hall brought in another group of super recruits, led by Lexington's own stars Jack "Goose" Givens and James Lee, as well as 6-foot-10 twin towers Rick Robey and Mike Phillips.

The arrival of Robey and Phillips quickly solved the depth problem at the center position. The new freshman recruits melded with the Super Kittens to create one of the most talented teams in the country.

After wins over Northwestern and Miami of Ohio, No. 15 Kentucky faced a highly anticipated matchup with No.3 Indiana at Bloomington. There they would weather one of the worst defeats in school history, 98-74. All-Americans Kent Benson and Scott May led the way for Indiana with 26 points and 25 points, respectively.

"[Indiana's coach] Bobby Knight rubbed it in," Grevey says of the loss. "He kept his starters in. [Coach Hall] said, 'Hey, Bobby! How much do you want to rub this in?'" Grevey recalls. "Knight yelled back, 'Shut up, Joe! You coach your team, and I'll coach mine.'"

After meeting with a referee to argue over a call, Grevey says Hall turned with the intention of returning to the UK bench. And then, Knight hit the UK coach. "Knight slapped [Coach Hall] on the back of the head, and his glasses came off," Grevey says. "We couldn't believe it."

Knight later said the slap was meant as a playful gesture. The Wildcats felt otherwise. "Coach Hall told us to remember it," Grevey says. "He said that he didn't know if we'd ever get an opportunity to get them back, but that if we did, we'd be ready."

\* \* \*

After the infuriating defeat, the Wildcats ran off to a 22-4 record, a share of the SEC Championship, and a birth in the NCAA's Mideast Regional—the same region as Indiana. After two victories, the fifth-ranked Wildcats earned their rematch with Indiana, and they were prepared for the contest.

"Coach Hall was brilliant at making adjustments, and we were never more ready for a game than we were for that one," Grevey says. "We knew we had to be physical with them, and we all said that if we played them again, we were all going to foul out of the game. So we ran through their picks, and we told the officials when they would foul. We didn't let them bully us. The plan worked. They began to foul us, and we stayed with them the whole game."

And in the end, paced by Mike Flynn—a 1971 Indiana Mr. Basketball—who scored 22 points, and Grevey, who scored 17 points, Kentucky advanced to the Final Four with a 92-90 victory. "That was by far the most satisfying win of my career," Grevey says. "They were awful, awful good. It was payback. It was a great revenge game. We thought we were champions after that game."

In the Final Four, Kentucky whipped Syracuse 95-79. On the other side of the bracket, UCLA scored a 75-74 overtime victory over Louisville, spoiling an interstate rivalry game for the national title.

"We really wanted to play Louisville, and they gave their game away to UCLA," Grevey says. "After we'd found out we were playing UCLA, we knew we were better than them. We thought we'd have a much easier game against UCLA than Louisville. So right there, we lost our edge."

Kentucky was deeper and more experienced than UCLA. To a man, Grevey says, the Wildcats were more talented. The national championship was within reach.

# THE GAME OF MY LIFE
### NCAA CHAMPIONSHIP:
### NO. 1 UCLA 92, NO. 2 KENTUCKY 85
### MARCH 31, 1975
### BY KEVIN GREVEY

I've held a grudge against John Wooden all these years. I'll never forget it. It was Easter Sunday, and our team was at the San Diego Zoo on our off day before the national championship. I was riding around with my brother on a train taking a tour of the zoo, and the press was following us around.

As we walked out of the zoo, they came up and told us the news: John Wooden, the legendary UCLA coach, was retiring. My jaw just dropped. Coach Hall immediately told us this wasn't going to make a difference in the game. But everyone was now looking at UCLA as America's favorite.

Before Wooden's announcement, people were tired of UCLA winning championships. Until then, they wanted Kentucky to win. But suddenly, things changed. UCLA was everyone's favorite. Everyone wanted to see Wooden go out a winner.

His retirement was a selfish thing, I think. He took the spotlight and put it on him before his team played in the championship, and that's not what I was taught. You don't call attention to yourself. Wooden's teachings were so eloquent, but this seemed to go against them.

* * *

The game was, by far, the biggest I'd played in. And early in the game, their big guys intimidated Robey and Phillips, our freshmen. As great as our freshmen were, they came out really flat in that game. Along with Givens and Lee, the freshmen didn't do much, and I could see it happening.

That's why I started forcing things, and I ended up with 34 points. That probably didn't help anything. I missed a lot of open shots and didn't have my best game. All this and their perimeter defense wasn't that great. They did a great job blocking shots, though.

The guy who killed us was the MVP, Richard Washington [28 points]. It was our lack of defense and rebounding that really hurt us, and those were the things we'd been doing all season long. In the end, we didn't do enough, and you just come away feeling awful. You feel like a loser.

They played a great game. But if we played ten times in Pauley Pavilion [UCLA's gym], we would have won eight of those. It was so disheartening. To be beat by a team that wasn't as good as you—that was hard. With one-game eliminations, you don't have those opportunities come along very often.

### Statline:

| MIN | FG | FGA | FT | FTA | REB | PTS |
|-----|----|----|----|-----|-----|-----|
| 36 | 13 | 30 | 8 | 10 | 5 | 34 |

# THE RESULT

Kentucky lost the national title, and Hall would have to wait three more seasons for his outstanding freshmen to bring home the championship.

Grevey led the team in scoring with 34 points, but the Wildcats could not combat the Bruins' tandem of Richard Washington, Dave Meyers, who scored 24, and Pete Trgovich, who scored 16 points. Each of the three played all 40 minutes in the game. Robey and Phillips finished with just six combined points and nine fouls. Flynn added 10 points for the Wildcats, but UCLA outrebounded UK 55-49.

"To say I thought we would win [the title] back then would be stretching a point," Wooden told Gordon S. White of *The New York Times*. Then again, it was Wooden's tenth title in 12 years.

"It took me a full summer to get over that loss," says Grevey, who averaged 23.6 points as a senior. "It was the most disappointing, most devastating loss I've ever felt in my career."

# AFTER BLUE

Following his college basketball career, Grevey was drafted by the NBA's Washington Bullets. After two seasons, he became a starter, averaging more than 15 points per game. Fueled by the Wildcats' defeat in the 1975 title contest, Grevey helped lead the Bullets to the world championship.

"It was a dream," he says. "Even though I really didn't start dreaming it until I was in college."

In 1978, Kentucky won its fifth national title. "I cried like a baby when Kentucky won the championship," he says. "Then we went on to win the world championship. Then I met my wife. Even to this day, if I see something with a '78' on it, like a bottle of wine or something, I buy it."

Today, after a decade in the NBA and a broadcasting career, Grevey owns a restaurant outside Washington, D.C., appropriately named Grevey's. He lives in Virginia with his wife and three children. In his restaurant, he displays memorabilia from his entire career—defeats and victories.

"Sometimes you have horrible disappointments in life," he says. "Was the loss in the title game a tragedy? No. It was just a failure. But you learn from these things. You become resilient.

"The wins are great," he says, "but the losses are where you learn."

# CHAPTER 9

# RICK ROBEY

It was 1974. Rick Robey was busy winning a state basketball championship for Brother Martin High School. He was named Louisiana's Mr. Basketball and a Parade All-American, and he had narrowed his college choices to Florida—his father's alma mater—as well as Notre Dame and Kentucky.

The Wildcats had the potential to be the nation's No. 1 team for the 1974-75 season. They were also putting together a stellar recruiting class. Playing time could be hard to come by, but Robey didn't care.

"I felt like there was a real good senior nucleus at Kentucky, and when those seniors were gone, we could be the next great senior nucleus," Robey says. "I felt like it was the perfect time to go there. When it came to minutes, I figured I'd either be good enough to play or I wouldn't be."

## THE SETTING

It was nearly a storybook finish for Robey during his freshman season. Kentucky needed bulk up front to complement scorers Kevin Grevey, Jimmy Dan Conner, and Mike Flynn. Coach Hall found it in the forms of the "Twin Towers"—Robey and fellow 6-foot-10 big man Mike Phillips. Also joining the outstanding recruiting class was Lexington's own famous duo: scorer Jack Givens and slashing sixth man James Lee.

The Twin Towers and the subs meshed well with the older players. UK had scoring, leadership, and strong bodies in the post. They ran off to a 26-5 record, an SEC championship, and a spot in the NCAA title game. But the Wildcats' big men were outplayed in a 92-85 loss to No. 1 UCLA during legendary coach John Wooden's final game.

* * *

Robey won a gold medal that summer with America's team in the Pan-Am Games in Mexico City. Over the next two seasons at Kentucky, the Wildcats posted a record of 46-14, won the 1976 NIT title, and tied for the conference championship in 1977 before falling to fifth-ranked North Carolina for a spot in the Final Four.

As a junior, Robey averaged 14.2 points per game, just behind Givens' 18.9-point average. Along with Lee and Phillips, the four-some was ready for a spectacular senior year and a No. 1 preseason ranking.

"We were, by that time, a great team," Robey says. "We were focused. We were really experienced, and we could beat teams in a number of ways."

They began the season 14-0, and after losing two of five games (one in overtime at LSU), the Wildcats went undefeated for the remainder of the regular season. As they approached Senior Day, an emotional event in which the seniors play their last game in front of the home crowd at Rupp Arena, the Wildcats had a sparkling 23-2 record as well as the nation's No. 1 ranking.

On Senior Day, the Wildcats faced unranked UNLV—a rare non-conference opponent. While the Runnin' Rebels had not yet cracked the nation's top 25, their lineup included Reggie Theus, an amazingly versatile player.

For Robey, Phillips, Givens, and Lee, it did not matter who they played. "The last time you're playing in front of that home crowd, you start thinking about everything you and your teammates have been through," Robey says. "This was our last go-around. You want to go out and have a great game—and we just manhandled them."

The magic of Senior Night, or—if the game is played in the after-noon—Senior Day, is familiar to Kentuckians. In 1978, NBC decid-

---

Rick Robey won championships in high school, college, and professional basketball.

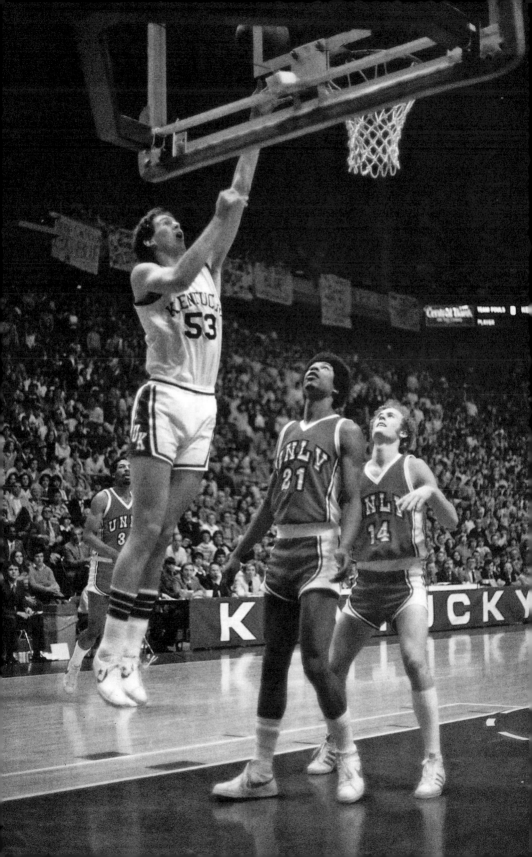

ed to broadcast the celebratory game. Included in their production were the pregame ceremonies associated with Senior Day. The late Happy Chandler led the sellout crowd in the singing of Stephen Foster's "My Old Kentucky Home" as the seniors and the parents made their way to center court. Many people in the crowd wept; the players tried to keep their emotions in check.

The power of the scene even affected the analysts, Dick Enberg and legendary coach and color man Al McGuire. "That's one of the most powerful scenes I've ever witnessed," Enberg said on the air. McGuire said that Senior Day alone "made Kentucky the nation's premiere basketball program."

In his book, *Full-Court Pressure*, Rick Pitino said that Kentucky's rivals complained to NBC, claiming the airing of the Senior Day ceremony gave Kentucky an unfair recruiting edge. And, Pitino noted, "They were right."

The last game at Rupp Arena capped an amazing regular season for the four seniors—a season which many contested the players were unable to enjoy because of the unbelievable pressure to win a national championship.

# THE GAME OF MY LIFE
## NO. 1 KENTUCKY 92, UNLV 70
### MARCH 4, 1978
### BY RICK ROBEY

You really couldn't have asked for a better sendoff for the four of us. We all went out and had great games. It typified our senior class. This was a nationally televised game, and it was a night we'd all remember.

All of my family was there. It was a packed house for the game. And it was so emotional during the ceremony. You start thinking about your career, because you've put all your heart and effort into that program. It makes you think about how fast those four years went. And then you think about how those years really propelled us to that point, where we were poised to win a national championship. It was one of those types of nights you wish wouldn't end.

I don't think we ever thought the game was really ever in doubt. But it was close through the first half [Kentucky led 40-39 at the half]. We took that emotion and really ran with it. I think each of the seniors ended up having a dunk in the game.

By golly, we were playing really perfectly at that time. It was a rare team where each senior knew his role, and we were executing really, really well. Looking back on it, all I really remember is how much we wanted to win.

As freshmen, we'd made it to the title game. As sophomores, I hurt my knee, and we won the NIT. As juniors, we lost to North Carolina and their four corners offense. But this was our year and our team. And being picked to win the title—that whole season was a dream come true.

I chose to come to Kentucky because I thought we had good leadership and that some day I'd be a part of a senior class that would be a group of good leaders, and I was right. It really did work out that way.

On Senior Day, we came out and played close in the first half and blew them out in the second half. We played well against Theus [he scored just 12 points], and we executed our game like we wanted to.

By the time it was over, we knew we'd never play in Rupp Arena in college again. But I was the MVP of the game. I went out with a great game and that felt really good.

### Statline:

| MIN | FG | FGA | FT | FTA | REB | A | PTS |
|-----|-----|-----|-----|-----|-----|-----|-----|
| 32 | 10 | 13 | 6 | 7 | 7 | 2 | 26 |

# THE RESULT

Robey finished with 26 points and seven rebounds. It was one of his best games as a Wildcat. Givens added 24 points, and Lee contributed 13 points. UNLV's Tony Smith scored 29 points for the Rebels.

The win perpetuated Kentucky's momentum, and the Wildcats entered the NCAA Tournament as the favorite. After wins against ranked opponents Florida State, Miami of Ohio, Michigan State, and Arkansas, Kentucky outplayed a lesser-talented Duke squad for a 94-88 victory in the national championship game. Givens scored 41 points, and Robey chipped in 20 points and 11 rebounds to bring home the school's fifth national title.

It had been 20 years since the school had won the NCAA crown. "We felt so good for us, for coach [Joe B.] Hall, and for the people across the state," Robey says. "That was what we had set as our goal for the season. It was an amazing feeling."

At last, Robey had an NCAA championship ring to add to his trophy case.

# AFTER BLUE

In 1978, Robey was the No. 3 pick in the NBA Draft by the Indiana Pacers. And in 1979, the Pacers traded Robey to the Boston Celtics, where he played alongside legendary forward Larry Bird.

Over the course of his NBA career, Robey averaged 7.6 points per game and 4.7 rebounds per game. He was a member of the Celtics in 1981 when Bird's Boston team won the world championship.

Louisiana State Title? Check. NCAA championship? Check. NBA world championship? Check.

After eight seasons in the NBA, Robey retired. He and his family moved back to Kentucky, where he obtained his real estate license. But his Kentucky basketball fame still transcends whatever he may accomplish in his professional life.

"Everyday, wherever you go, you run into a Kentucky fan," Robey says. "And they always say the same thing: 'I hate bothering you about this, but...' and they want to talk about the 1978 team. Heck, that's fun. That's what it's all about. I love talking to the fans about all of this stuff. That was an incredible time."

# CHAPTER 10

# KYLE MACY

As strange as it may seem, some of Kentucky basketball's brightest stars have come from the neighboring—and sometimes loathed—state of Indiana. Walter McCarty was one, and Mike Flynn was another. But few Kentucky players were more popular than Kyle Macy, who also hailed from the Hoosier state. And when he finally became a Wildcat in 1977, he was the missing piece of a puzzle that was five years in the making.

Fans still talk of Macy's characteristic free throw routine: he would always dry his hands on his socks before he shot from the charity stripe. "It's about a routine," he says. "Everyone needs to have their routine, their rhythm from the line."

Macy made about nine out of every ten free throws. It aroused superstition and relief when he actually *missed* from the line. "Because I knew then I'd gotten the one miss out of the way," he says.

And that aura of superstition would follow him and his well-known routine throughout his athletic career—from Peru High School, where he set a state scoring mark and earned the title of Mr. Basketball, to Purdue University, where he played during his freshman season.

After a wildly productive season in which he scored 18 points in his first game and 38 points in his first conference game, Macy wanted a change of scenery; and after looking at several schools, he decided he wanted to play for Kentucky. He believed he could offer the steady point guard play the Wildcats needed, and Kentucky could challenge for a national title.

But there was one problem: Kentucky didn't accept transfers. "I really had to sell myself to Coach Hall," Macy says. After watching Macy play, Hall realized the former Boilermaker was too talented to pass up.

After sitting out a transfer year, Kyle Macy was eligible for the 1977-78 season. The timing was ideal. Powerful guard Larry Johnson was gone, and Hall's outstanding recruits from 1974 were seniors. It would be the Wildcats' last chance to get back to the Final Four after their championship loss in 1975.

# THE SETTING

Coming into the 1977-78 season, the Wildcats were a unanimous selection to win the national championship. The Indiana Hoosiers' run seemed to be waning, and the Wildcats had depth, bulk, quickness, experience, and deadly shooters.

The media predicted that fans would be unsatisfied with Hall and the team unless they won the national championship. Thus, the year became known as "The Season Without Joy."

"The media made our team out to be known as the team without fun," Macy says, "but that really wasn't the case." After all, it's always fun when you're winning.

With Macy running point, the Wildcats began the season 14-0.

The team went undefeated until its 15th game, when they lost to Alabama. The next loss came four games later in overtime at LSU. Then, an impressive 10-game winning streak ensued.

Along the way, the Wildcats won the SEC Championship, earned a No. 1 seed in the NCAA Tournament, and defeated 13th-ranked Florida State and 19th-ranked Miami of Ohio en route to the NCAA regional final.

But Michigan State awaited Kentucky, led by their outstanding freshman guard, Ervin Johnson. Later, Ervin would become known as "Magic." But in 1978, Kyle Macy would get the better of Magic.

# THE GAME OF MY LIFE
## NCAA MIDEAST REGIONAL FINAL:
### NO. 1 KENTUCKY 52, NO. 4 MICHIGAN STATE 49
### MARCH 18, 1978
### BY KYLE MACY

I was so lucky to be a part of that team. We could really win

Kyle Macy was one of several stars from Indiana who had stellar careers as Wildcats.

games in any way. If a team wanted to slow it down, we could get it inside to our big men. If we were playing a team who wanted to run, we could run and shoot. We were one of the best teams in history because of that.

Michigan State had an athletic team, and they played a matchup zone. We wanted to slow it up and run our offense.

It was a close game in the first half, and a lot of people, and some in the media, speculated that we would succumb to the pressure of a close game. But we didn't—we executed our offense. In the first half, we got down [Michigan State led 27-22].

It was good though for me, because I missed my first free throw in the game. When I missed that first one, I thought, 'Good.' I'd gotten the miss out of the way, so I figured I'd make the rest.

At halftime, it took our coaches to make an adjustment. Coach Hall called me over and said we'd run a high pick with Rick Robey and me. We'd watch what the defense did and react to that.

In the second half, that's what we did, and Michigan State's guys would always switch on Robey, leaving me open and leaving Goose Givens open on the wing. That led to me driving and getting fouled a lot, and down the stretch I was able to go to the line and knock down my free throws. That's when I hit 10 in a row; I didn't miss again after that first miss.

You always feel nervous when you're playing in a big game, and when you're on the line, possibly with the game in the balance, you're a little more nervous. And this wasn't any game—this was to go to the Final Four.

But you always feel better when you've practiced something and you've done it before. So I had my routine: I'd dry my hands on my socks. I kept doing that, and my free throws kept going in. And we were able to do what a lot of people said we couldn't—we won a close game. That got us a spot in the Final Four.

**Statline:**

| MIN | FG | FGA | FT | FTA | A | PTS |
|-----|-----|-----|-----|-----|-----|-----|
| 40 | 4 | 10 | 10 | 11 | 2 | 18 |

# THE RESULT

Macy's performance at the free-throw line during the last few minutes of the NCAA regional final game earned him the nickname "Cool Kyle."

"Macy . . . scored nine points—all but two of them from the free throw line—in the last 6:16 of the game," reported *The New York Times*. Kentucky won by just three points, making each of Macy's 10 free throws all the more important. He played all 40 minutes for the Wildcats, who took their first lead on two Phillips' free throws with 7:02 to play. Givens chipped in 14 points, and Mike Phillips scored 10 points.

For the Spartans, Johnson finished with six points (far below his 17.4 points per game average) and five assists; but he also turned the ball over six times and was whistled for four fouls. Greg Kelser scored 19 points, and Bob Chapman added 10 points.

And Macy says he didn't even get a piece of the championship net during the postgame celebration. "I was immediately rushed after the game to talk to Greg Gumbel," he says. "No one got me a piece of the net."

After the Wildcats defeated Arkansas in the national semifinal, they beat Duke 94-88 to win the school's fifth national championship—and the first championship in 20 years. "We did exactly what we wanted to do," Macy says. "And for all of those people who said it was a season without joy, we think it was the most joyous season we could've had."

* * *

Macy led the Wildcats during Kentucky's rebuilding season the next year. Ranked tenth in the early season, Kentucky faced No. 5 Kansas in a December game in Rupp Arena. Down 66-60 with 31 seconds left in overtime, cat-quick guard Dwight Anderson scored a layup to bring Kentucky within four points of Kansas. After getting the ball back, Anderson was fouled with 16 seconds left on the clock. He missed the front end of a bonus free throw, which caused a melee. But Anderson retrieved the ball and was again fouled. This time he made both free throws, and Kentucky trailed by two points.

After Kansas in-bounded the ball, Anderson knocked it loose from the Jayhawks' Mac Stallcup. Macy picked it up and stroked a 15-foot jumper for the tie. After the shot, Kansas guard Darnell Valentine signaled for a timeout.

There was only one problem—Kansas had no timeouts remaining. The Jayhawks were tagged with a technical foul. Once again, with the game on the line, Macy nailed the game-winning technical free throw as the Wildcats escaped 67-66.

But Kentucky could not get lucky in every game. The Wildcats finished with a record of 19-12 and lost to Clemson in the first round of the NIT.

During Macy's senior season, the Kentucky team reloaded with freshman star Sam Bowie at center. The Wildcats went 29-6, won the SEC Championship and the Great Alaska Shootout, and returned to the NCAA Tournament. But Kentucky, again ranked No. 1, lost to 14th-ranked Duke in the regional, 55-54. Macy's career was over, but few Wildcats were more beloved.

# AFTER BLUE

Drafted No. 22 in the first round by Phoenix, Macy played seven seasons in the NBA, bouncing between Phoenix, Chicago, and Indiana. Along the way, he became one of the early backcourt mates of Michael Jordan in Chicago. His productive professional career left him with averages of 9.5 points and four assists per game.

After serving as a broadcaster for Kentucky basketball for several years, Macy coached at Morehead State for nine seasons. He led the Eagles to a 20-win season in 2003, when they won a share of the Ohio Valley Conference title. But Macy resigned after a poor start in 2006.

Now he's working as a broadcaster in Kentucky again, where he lives with his wife, his two daughters, and his son. He's even thinking of establishing a youth basketball camp to help children with their free-throw shooting.

He still wears his championship ring, he says, and few days go by without a Kentucky fan asking about 1978. "I couldn't have written a better script," Macy says. "The way it all turned out was the best thing that could've happened."

# CHAPTER 11

# JACK GIVENS

Few—if any—Kentucky players from Lexington have been as heralded as Jack "Goose" Givens, a left-handed shooting marvel from Bryan Station High School. They called him "Goose" because his game was reminiscent of Harlem Globetrotter Goose Tatum. Once in high school, he scored 45 points against his rival, James Lee of Henry Clay High School. Somewhere during those years, Givens says, the nickname stuck.

But despite his love for the state of Kentucky and the city of Lexington, he wasn't a UK fan. "Obviously, at that time, there weren't a lot of African-Americans at UK," Givens says. "But as I kept getting older, I got a chance to follow UK basketball a bit. Things started to change."

People from across Kentucky wrote him letters, begging him to attend the state's largest school. "It made the decision a little easier to go through," Givens says.

Then again, deciding where to go to college is a tough decision for anyone. And Givens had never even flown on an airplane before.

"Getting on [a plane] to go and visit other schools, I just didn't do that," Givens says. "I never visited anywhere. I went to [Eastern Kentucky University], and I went down to look at the University of Tennessee. UCLA wanted me, and UNLV wanted me, but they were too far away. I knew that Kentucky was the best place for me to be."

After Givens' senior year, during which he earned the Mr. Basketball honor, he became an important member of one of

Kentucky's most talented recruiting classes. Joining Givens were inside threats Rick Robey and Mike Phillips, along with another Lexington native—Givens' rival James Lee.

# THE SETTING

As UK welcomed new recruits Givens, Robey, Phillips, and Lee to campus, the basketball program was poised to enter a dynastic period. Traditional national power UCLA's seemingly annual hold on the national championship was nearing an end, and Kentucky and Indiana, among others, were making their own claims to the title.

After a 13-13 season in 1974, Kentucky basketball was hurting, primarily due to a lack of size—although leading scorer Kevin Grevey still provided 20-plus points per game. The Wildcats were searching for tall, talented players.

In 1974-75, the Wildcats were again title contenders. Kevin Grevey and Jimmy Dan Conner were leading scorers, and Robey and Phillips provided the bulk in the frontcourt. But Kentucky fell just short of the title, as UCLA coach John Wooden announced his retirement the day before the championship game. In Wooden's last game, the Bruins captured their tenth title, defeating an athletically superior Wildcats team, 92-85.

Kevin Grevey and his fellow seniors would have to leave without a championship. In 1976, a rebuilding year, someone had to step up and fill Grevey's high-scoring shoes.

That "someone" would be Goose Givens, who dropped in more than 20 points per game, leading a scrappy group of Wildcats to a 16-10 record and a birth in the NIT tournament. After wins over Niagara, Kansas State, and Providence, the Wildcats brought another championship to Lexington with a 71-67 win over Charlotte.

But Givens and the recruits wanted something more. They wanted to win the SEC and capture the school's fifth national title.

During Givens' junior year, the team began to assert its dominance— with help from sophomore guard Truman Claytor. Early-season demolitions of fourth-ranked Indiana (66-51) and second-ranked Notre Dame (102-78) sent a message to the rest of the coun-

---

Jack Givens saved his best game for the biggest stage – 41 points against Duke in the NCAA title contest.

try: Watch out for the Wildcats. After winning the SEC, Kentucky carried the nation's No. 6 ranking into NCAA Tournament play.

Wins over Princeton and VMI set up a classic matchup with fifth-ranked North Carolina. But the Tar Heels proved too much to handle in a 79-72 loss in the East Regional finals. Again, Goose Givens was denied a title. But perhaps most frustratingly, the Wildcats were finding it difficult to get back to the Final Four. Help would come from the unlikeliest of places—Indiana.

* * *

Point guard Kyle Macy, a transfer from Purdue, was ready to break into the starting lineup. The sophomore brought composure and leadership that meshed perfectly with the team. But the Wildcats still belonged to Robey and Givens.

The 1977-78 Wildcats began the season as the nation's No. 2 ranked squad; but they took the top ranking in early December, and they would hold onto it for more than two months.

The seniors led the way—Givens scoring 18 points per game and Robey 14 points per game. Macy ran the team with poise and contributed over 12 points per game. Early wins over No. 19 Kansas (73-66) and No. 4 Notre Dame (73-68) gave the Wildcats' confidence for the conference schedule. Kentucky finished the regular season 25-2, 16-2 in the SEC, and entered the NCAA Tournament—again ranked No. 1.

After a close win in Knoxville over Florida State (85-76), the Wildcats ran through Miami, Ohio (91-69), and narrowly defeated Magic Johnson and Michigan State (52-49) with the help of Macy's clutch free throws down the stretch. Givens was named the region's Most Outstanding Player.

Another suspenseful victory over Arkansas (64-59) earned the Wildcats seniors a trip to their dream game. They would face No. 7 Duke in the championship game. The Blue Devils, led by Mike Gminski, Jim Spanarkel, and Gene Banks, were formidable.

Three years earlier, the Wildcats seniors had played UCLA and lost. Now, they would get a second chance. "We had that experience," Givens says. "We knew what it was like to go and lose, and we didn't want that feeling again."

# THE GAME OF MY LIFE
## NCAA CHAMPIONSHIP:
## NO. 1 KENTUCKY 94, NO. 7 DUKE 88
## MARCH 27, 1978
### BY JACK GIVENS

The first thing I remember about that game was that before it even started, there was a confidence and a comfort level that I had going into it. It was something different than I had felt in any other game. Other than that, I can't really explain it.

There were some games when I was a freshman and I wasn't expected to contribute very much. I felt calm sometimes then, but this was our biggest game—the national championship game—and I really felt calm, like there was no pressure. This was our opportunity as seniors to do what we wanted to do. I was the leading scorer and the captain, but this was not pressure, this was an opportunity. We were prepared mentally and physically going into that game. We felt we were the better team, and we were confident.

The game started like we thought it would—both teams feeling each other out. But we never lost that confidence. We were able to do what we were supposed to do, and things got easier. It was like the whole season. We knew our jobs, and Coach Hall turned the team over to us—and we did it. As the season wore on, our philosophy was: "If we do the things we're capable of doing, we don't have to worry about the other team."

We knew every player they had and what they did. We were a defensive-minded team, playing a 1-3-1 zone and a man-to-man. We really had no weaknesses. We had big guys, scorers, shooters, and a deep bench. James Lee was just like another starter for us. We knew we had a deeper team than Duke, and we knew we had more experience having played in the finals before. While everyone else was happy to be there, we were there to win it.

We knew we had to win the game physically with defense, with Robey and Phillips down low. And we knew they had a lot to worry about. In the game, we knew Robey and Phillips would take attention on the inside and open things up for Truman and Macy on the outside. And the scorers could then score.

My shot was the mid-range jumper, the 15-20 foot jumper, and the 8-18 foot jumper. That was my shot my whole career, and that shot was open all night. I also worked on getting putbacks around the hoop.

But as the first half kept going, I was getting on a roll. It got to a point where I wasn't concerned about shot selection. I started making so many shots. I had 16 [of the team's final 18] points to end the first half. In the last minute, I put in a shot. Then we got the ball back and I hit one in the corner. Then I took a charge and hit two free throws to end the half. Our offense was going, and we were making shots. I didn't even have to think. I remember we were only up by about seven at the half. It seemed they had hit a lot of free throws to keep them in it.

In the locker room at halftime, we were anxious to get back out there. We had taken control and wanted to get back out and play. There was no motivation needed, and Coach Hall knew he didn't have to say anything. There was nothing he could say that we hadn't already heard.

In the second half, I came out the same way. I was looking for the ball. A lot of people remember the shot I hit from the baseline—I banked it high off the top of the glass, and it fell through. It just grazed the backboard.

When a shot like that goes through, as a player, you think, "Well, OK, that's a bonus." Then you want to get your next shot and ride that feeling as long as you can. Fortunately, my shots continued to be there, and I kept hitting them.

It ended up looking like a closer game than it really was, because Coach Hall took all the veterans out and Duke made some shots. But we always felt like we were in control. I don't want to take anything away from Duke—they were a good team. There was no quit in them.

James Lee got to end the game with a big dunk, which was fitting to end our careers like that. He deserved a lot more credit than he might've gotten.

When we got back to the airport the next day, there were thousands of people cheering, welcoming us back. We felt like we'd done what we wanted to do, and we got a championship for Coach Hall.

## Statline:

| MIN | FG | FGA | FT | FTA | REB | PTS |
|-----|-----|-----|-----|-----|-----|-----|
| 37 | 18 | 27 | 5 | 8 | 8 | 41 |

# THE RESULT

Hall's famed recruiting class of 1974 had delivered his first—and it would turn out to be only—national title. "The pressure's been on six seasons, really," Hall told Paul Borden of the Louisville *Courier-Journal.* At that point, it had been six seasons since he'd taken over for legendary coach Adolph Rupp in 1972.

While some would later refer to the 1978 campaign as "A Season Without Joy," because the pressure to win was so apparent, Givens says the only joy that mattered was the feeling he and his teammates shared when hoisting up the championship trophy.

"It was the ultimate team," Givens says. "You can look at each of our games throughout the NCAA Tournament, and you can see how a different player, or a different group of players, stepped up to help earn a win."

Givens saved his best performance for last. His 41 points were the third-most recorded in a title game, bested only by Bill Walton's 44 in 1973 and Gail Goodrich's 42 in 1965—both for UCLA.

"I noticed Coach was trying to get me the ball as time was winding down, and he really hadn't done that much," Givens says. "That's when I knew I'd scored a lot. He was trying to get me the record."

Robey chipped in 20 points and 11 rebounds, while Macy had nine points and eight assists. But Givens would go on to earn the cover of that week's *Sports Illustrated.*

Duke's players, though young, also played big. Starting a junior, two sophomores, and two freshmen, the Blue Devils refused to fold—even while down as much as 16 points in the first half. Banks scored 22 points and grabbed eight rebounds, while Gminski added 20 points and 12 rebounds. Spanarkel scored 21 points. It was the beginning of what would become a fabled Kentucky/Duke rivalry.

"No one knew it then," Givens says. "But this was kind of the first game in that. Everyone always wants to see Kentucky and Duke play each other. We kind of got that started."

# AFTER BLUE

Givens became known as the Wildcat who gave the most magnificent performance on the grandest stage. He did not know it then, but for the rest of his life, he would be a hero in the Bluegrass State.

When his playing career was over, Givens was drafted No. 16 by

Atlanta in the first round. Givens played merely two seasons in the NBA. "It was good and fun, but it was not what I expected to be," Givens says. "Back then, the NBA was big, but it wasn't what it is now. It definitely wasn't as glorified as my college career."

Now, after stints as a color analyst with the Orlando Magic and other television outlets, Givens works as a real estate agent in Florida. And even today, he says, people approach him to talk about his big game in 1978.

"It's amazing," Givens says. "There are a lot of people, even now, that remember the game like it was yesterday. I still receive stuff in the mail from fans. People want me to sign the *Sports Illustrated* cover.

"To have a game like that in the finals, as the last game of your college career, that's a wonderful feeling," he says. "That means you've won the championship. That's what it's all about."

# CHAPTER 12

# SAM BOWIE

From the moment Sam Bowie stepped off the plane in the Bluegrass State, he knew he wanted to be a Kentucky Wildcat. "I was on my official visit to the campus," Bowie says, "and when I walked into the airport, there were about 3,000 fans there to welcome me. I'll never forget how I went back home and told my mom and dad that story. I knew Kentucky was the place for me."

At the time, Bowie was the most sought-after recruit in the country—possibly the most sought-after recruit in Kentucky history. And it wasn't difficult to see why. At 7-foot-1, Sam Bowie was not only one of the tallest players in the nation, but also one of the most versatile. Possessing great leaping ability and touch, Bowie was teeming with raw talent, averaging 28 points and 18 rebounds per game for Lebanon High School in Pennsylvania. He could use his post moves down low or step out to hit a mid-range jumper. He would go on to earn *Parade* and McDonald's All-American honors for his efforts.

Bowie was the kind of impact player who could immediately produce for a team. He was especially welcome at Kentucky, which had lacked height since the 1978 national championship team.

After a fiercely competitive recruiting process, his decision came down to one spectacular moment. "The crowd, just coming out to welcome a recruit at the airport, that was amazing," Bowie says. "It was obvious these people cared about basketball."

# THE SETTING

Bowie was an instant success during his first season as a Wildcat. He scored 22 points and pulled down 17 rebounds in his debut against Duke. Along with the other members of his talented recruiting class—Dirk Minniefield, Derrick Hord, and Charles Hurt—the team proved it was once again formidable and ready to make a run at the Final Four.

Bowie averaged 12.9 points and 8.1 rebounds as freshman. The team posted a record of 28-5 and reached No.3 in country, only to lose to Duke in the second round of the NCAA Tournament, 55-54. To make matters worse, the game was held at Rupp Arena.

During Bowie's sophomore season, the team went 22-6 but lost to UAB in the NCAA first round, 69-62. Bowie averaged 17.4 points and 9.1 rebounds as a sophomore, earning All-America honors.

With two consecutive years of being upset in the NCAA tournament, Kentucky fans would normally have seemed disgruntled. But this was a time of great optimism. Coach Joe B. Hall was recruiting well, and the returning Kentucky team would surely challenge for a national title for many years to come. Bowie was poised to be UK's best big man ever.

\* \* \*

But before the beginning of his junior year, Bowie broke his leg. He would be sidelined for the entire season. And his unfortunate injury drastically changed the team. Although the Wildcats showcased a talented roster, the squad would greatly miss its 7-foot-1 catalyst. And the news worsened: Bowie was forced to miss a second season. His stress fracture did not heal properly and required bone-graft surgery.

"That was the toughest time, realizing I would have to miss another full season," Bowie says.

In his absence, Kentucky went 22-8 and 23-8 but could not reach the Final Four. It is certain the Wildcats would have challenged for championships had Bowie been included in the lineup.

Soon, players like Kenny Walker arrived to help. It all added up

---

Sam Bowie (No. 31) was one of the most high-profile recruits in Kentucky history, and he helped lead the Wildcats to the 1984 Final Four.

to a magical season in which Kentucky had an abundance of talent and, at last, a healthy Sam Bowie.

But in 1983, Sam Bowie was simply one member of a very talented team. He was no longer the go-to guy. Senior Mel Turpin and sophomore Kenny Walker had supplanted Bowie as the team's scorers. It was now Bowie's role to lead, rebound, and provide an extra presence in the paint.

And joining the likes of Walker, Turpin, Bowie, Jim Master, and Dicky Beal were a pair of high-profile freshmen: Winston Bennett and James Blackmon. This Kentucky team had talent to spare.

After losing the first "Dream Game" to Louisville in the NCAA regional finals the previous season, an upgraded Kentucky team blasted the No.6 Cardinals 65-44 to open the season. The Wildcats won 12 straight games, climbing to No. 2 in the polls.

Coming into their last game, the team was 22-4, ranked No. 3 in the country, and leading the SEC by a game over LSU. If they defeated LSU on Senior Night, the Wildcats would clinch the SEC regular-season title. A loss would mean a tie with the Bayou Bengals, and Sam Bowie did not want a tie.

# THE GAME OF MY LIFE
## NO. 3 KENTUCKY 90, LSU 68
### MARCH 3, 1984
#### BY SAM BOWIE

It was Senior Night—my last game in Rupp Arena. Obviously, the emotions were flowing.

As far as the SEC went, Kentucky and LSU were the premiere teams in the league that season. We had a one-game lead on them for the conference title with one game to go, and it just so happened that we got to play them on Senior Night. We didn't want to share the title with them.

I knew that as far as I was concerned, I was really affected by the pageantry of 'it all. There's nothing like Senior Night at Kentucky. And for me, it probably meant a little more, because I'd been injured and lost those years, so I became even more attached to the area and the institution.

I kept breaking down numerous times before the game. It was a difficult thing just trying to get your emotions in order. You had to go from being an emotional wreck, basically, to getting your mind ready to play a big game. I mean—we were playing not only our last game at Rupp [Arena], but it was a game for a conference championship.

In the locker room before the game, there was a lot of cutting up among the seniors. Everyone wanted to know who was going to be the first one to shed a tear. There was a lot of goosebumps, and tears and emotion, especially when they played "My Old Kentucky Home."

Then they always have the seniors run through these huge hoops with your face on it. They saved me for last.

So I came out and ran through my hoop. I broke the paper with my face on it and came through—and I couldn't help it. I was concerned about my teammates seeing me break down, but there was nothing I could do. The rest of them could hold up, but with 24,000 fans there cheering, I was the first to break down.

It was all about the relationships you develop while you're at Kentucky. My mother was with me that day, but my father had passed away during my sophomore season. As I walked to center court, my mother was waiting for me. She said, 'I love you,' and she hugged me, and that's when I lost it.

With me and the other seniors—Mel Turpin, Jim Master, Dicky Beal, and Tom Heitz—we'd traveled a long road to get to that moment.

I was weeping by that point—that's a good way to say it.

* * *

Then we had to go back to warming up for the game. I went back to the team and a lot of people were kidding with me, saying things like, "I told you you'd break down." But I had to put all of that behind me. We had some LSU Tigers to deal with.

Dale Brown had a good team, but I'll never forget the opening play of that game. On the opening tip, I was able to tip it and we got the ball. Kenny Walker set a pick for me, because we used to open every ballgame with a lob for a dunk. So Dicky Beal looked to me for the lob, and he threw it up.

I felt like I could jump an extra six inches because of the emotion of that opening ceremony. I threw down the dunk and that really brought the crowd into it in a hurry.

But after that, it was nip and tuck the whole way through. Anytime you're playing LSU, it's a tough game. We ran out to a lead at the half [31-23] and during the break in the locker room, I did stop to think about my teammates. I looked across the room at the players and the coaches, and I thought this would be the last time I ever played with these teammates and coaches in this locker room again. I didn't want to lose.

Even though it was close in the second half, by the time we made our stretch run, LSU was running out of gas. I remember I was able to make several key plays down the stretch, and the crowd got into it, and before you knew it, we were up by double figures; and then we were up by about 20 points.

With less than a minute to go, I was taken out of the game. I just looked over, and I saw someone else was coming in for me. Then I looked to the rafters, thanked the good Lord for getting me healthy, and I realized I just couldn't believe it was over.

It's probably obvious that I'm an emotional type of guy. I hugged Coach Hall, went to the bench and put a towel over my head. And I just lost it, emotionally, for the second time that night.

## Statline:

| MIN | FG | FGA | FT | FTA | B | REB | PTS |
|-----|-----|-----|-----|-----|-----|-----|-----|
| 34 | 5 | 6 | 10 | 11 | 4 | 16 | 20 |

# THE RESULT

Bowie had a typical stat-filled game on Senior Night, with 20 points, 16 rebounds, and four blocks. Turpin scored 19 points, and Beal added 13 points. Master and Heitz both scored four points. The team clinched the SEC regular-season title and went on to claim the tournament title as well.

Then came Bowie's annual nemesis: The NCAA Tournament. Earning a bye, the Wildcats defeated BYU in the second round.

And, as it turned out, Senior Night wasn't the final time Bowie would take the court in front of his home crowd. Thanks to the NCAA's selection committee, Bowie played that year's NCAA regionals in Rupp Arena—although nothing could match the emotion of Senior Night.

The Wildcats again bested Louisville to reach a regional final showdown with sixth-ranked Illinois. A 54-51 win over the Illini sent the Wildcats to the Final Four for the first time since 1978.

"Some people would say their best game would be beating Illinois and earning a spot in the Final Four," Bowie says. "And that was a wonderful feeling."

But the dream ended there. The Wildcats suffered a nightmarish experience against Patrick Ewing and Georgetown. Kentucky should have won the game, but they shot a sickly 3-for-33 in the second half to lose, 53-40.

Nevertheless, after a long journey, Bowie had reached the Final Four and left his name in the UK record books. But fans will forever question what might have been had Sam Bowie been healthy for four consecutive seasons of UK basketball.

# AFTER BLUE

Today, it seems as if Bowie's name is eternally linked with jokes about the NBA Draft. After his senior season, Bowie was selected by the Portland Trailblazers as the second pick overall in the 1984 draft, just ahead of Michael Jordan, who was picked third by the Chicago Bulls.

In hindsight, it seems the Blazers made a poor choice. But a well-known saying in the NBA goes something like this: If you make a mistake in the draft, make it big. In other words, it's a good idea to draft big men, and if a tall draft pick doesn't pan out, so be it. Centers in the NBA are at a premium, and no one can fault a team for drafting an athletic center, a la Bowie.

Bowie went on to have a solid 10-year NBA career, but he was still hampered by injuries. He played in Portland, New Jersey, and Los Angeles before retiring in 1995. "I was blessed to make enough money for myself that I can be happy and do what I want," Bowie says.

Now, he lives in Lexington, where he aids UK in basketball radio broadcasts. He also breeds horses. But his favorite activity is watching his three children grow up. "There's nothing like it," he says.

And his favorite game will always be his Senior Night victory. "I'll always remember it," he says. "That's something that stays with you for all time."

# CHAPTER 13

# KENNY WALKER

They called him Sky—as in Sky-Walker. But Kenny Walker wasn't always big. And he couldn't always leap tall players in a single bound.

Walker grew up the youngest of four brothers on a peach farm in rural Roberta, Georgia. And when the boys would go out to practice their basketball skills, little Kenny—just five years old—wanted to play, too.

But sometimes his brothers wouldn't play fair. The older Walkers would swat his shot, or worse—not let him have the ball at all. They would talk trash; they would try to get in his head. "They would do some derogatory things," Walker remembers.

So his mother, Ola Walker, took an old peach basket, cut out the bottom, and—in a throwback to Dr. James Naismith himself—nailed the basket to a utility pole. That was Kenny's basket—the one where he could practice his shooting without anyone bothering him.

For hours a day, he honed a game that would become legendary. Sometimes his brothers would help him, teaching him some big boy skills. And other times they taunted him, teaching him to keep his emotions in check and focus on the game. It worked, and Kenny began to improve.

"He can ring it," Kenny's mother would say of his shooting skills. His shooting touch and height (Walker was 6-foot-2 in the ninth grade) earned him a spot on the junior varsity team at Crawford County as a ninth grader. And that led to the day when Walker dunked the basketball for the first time.

"I'd always tried to do it before," Walker says. "And I'd always jump and put the ball off the back rim of the basket. The ball would pop out." But this day would be different. As the team began practice, they split into two layup lines to warm up. Walker's coach was busy climbing a ladder, setting up some lights in the gymnasium. When it came time for Walker to score his layup, he tried to dunk again.

"I remember I reached down, and I got a little lower than normal," Walker says. "And when I got lower, I got a little bit more on my jump. And I just took off. And then I did it again. And again," he says. "I did it five times in a row. I was just jumping like I'd never done before. My teammates were high-fiving each other. And my coach, he got down off the ladder and was just like, 'Damn!'"

\* \* \*

After two state championships at Crawford County, Walker was ready for college basketball of the highest caliber. And when he stepped foot on Kentucky's campus, the 6-foot-8, 190-pound freshman made an immediate impact.

As a freshman, he averaged seven points per game for a team that won 23 games and an SEC championship before falling to Louisville 80-68 in the NCAA Mideast Regional Final. He then upped his average to 12.4 points per game as a sophomore for a UK team that won 29 games and reached the Final Four before losing to Georgetown, 53-40.

But Walker's junior year would prove to be the most trying. The team had lost senior towers Mel Turpin and Sam Bowie, as well as guard Jim Master. Several young Wildcats were learning their roles—including Winston Bennett and Ed Davender. And rumors hung in the air. Some thought Joe B. Hall may retire.

## THE SETTING

Joe B. Hall had an unenviable task. Coach Adolph Rupp had been larger than life. He developed a tradition where there was none. He won more games than any other and claimed four national championships. Rupp came from coaching royalty in Kansas and brought the game to the Bluegrass. But when Coach Rupp retired, Hall not

---

Kenny Walker led a rebuilding UK squad to a surprising Sweet
Sixteen run in 1985.

only kept the program running, he excelled.

Hall returned Kentucky to the top of the recruiting world. He delivered the long-awaited fifth national championship in 1978. He added eight conference titles and an NIT championship in 1976.

"Looking back, I'd have to say that Joe B. Hall did one helluva job," legendary broadcaster Cawood Ledford said in his autobiography *Hello Everybody, This is Cawood Ledford.*

In 1985, Hall was under investigation for more than 320 tickets he owned for games at Rupp Arena. Both the *Lexington Herald-Leader* and Louisville *Courier-Journal* newspapers were pursuing the story. Ledford said the investigation, and subsequent investigations into the UK program, weighed on Hall's mind. But no one knew for sure whether or not 1985 would he his last season.

\* \* \*

The 1984-1985 season was a rebuilding year, but few could have foreseen the Wildcats' 1-4 start. After a season-opening win over Toledo, the team lost to Purdue, SMU, Indiana, and Louisville. But Kentucky began to right the ship with wins over East Tennessee State and Cincinnati in the UK Invitational Tournament.

Kentucky had yet to find a consistent offense, and their young players were struggling to fit into the system. The team had potential, but it went unrealized until Danny Manning and No. 12 Kansas came to Louisville on New Year's Eve to face the unranked Wildcats in UK's annual game in Freedom Hall.

The Kentucky offense came alive, and Kenny Walker was the beneficiary. His game would go down as one of the greatest ever played by a Wildcat. And it would set the tone for the rest of the year.

# THE GAME OF MY LIFE
## KENTUCKY 92, NO. 11 KANSAS 89
### DECEMBER 31, 1984
### BY KENNY WALKER

That was the worst start to a season that we'd had at Kentucky in a long time. We were an inexperienced team, and we didn't know our roles. But a few days before the Kansas game, Coach Hall said we were going to change the offense—that we were going to run the offense more through me.

I remember, going into that game, that we really needed a signature win. We were 3-4 at that time, and we needed to show we could beat a good team. Kansas was a big name and a good team, and we wanted to play well. Kansas had a big 7-footer that was a difficult matchup for us. And another big athletic guard they had was really good. And then they had Danny Manning, and certainly at that time, no one knew how good he was going to be.

The good thing for me was the game was played in Freedom Hall. I think, and I think you'll hear this from a lot of other players, that Freedom Hall is a great place to play. It's not too big—it's just the right size—and I always felt comfortable there. The colors in the background are dark, not distracting, and you feel like you're on stage. And the rims—the rims in Rupp Arena are very tight, but the rims in Freedom Hall are soft. There were many shots that I put up in the Kansas game that hit the rim and bounced a few times and fell right through.

But before the game, we were energized. We came out more ready to play than in past games. Early and often my teammates got the ball to me. I was known as a leaper, and our guards could throw me the ball in spots where I could jump up and get it. I could hit turnaround jumpers from the baseline and jump hooks, and that's what I did.

But the way I really got a lot of points, and the way I put a lot of pressure on the guy guarding me, was I could run the floor. I would get back down court and get a lot of layups and dunks.

That game was the beginning of my teammates really having confidence in me as a scorer. They knew then that I could get the ball and do something with it. It was really the kind of night that every player dreams about.

But what I really remember most about that night was the number of free throws I missed. I learned early on that as a big man, if I could make free throws, I could get six or seven more points a game. And in that Kansas game, I should've scored about 40, but I missed those free throws.

I never was the type of guy who talked a lot during the game. I let my game do the talking on the court. And I never knew how many points I had. I knew I'd missed a lot of free throws, and that I rebounded well and that I played hard.

That was our first really big win over a big opponent. I mean, even though we were Kentucky, we weren't having the best year. But this game gave us the confidence—and gave me the confidence—that we could play and really do well against a big-time team. This was what we needed to get through the rest of the season.

## Statline:

| FG | FGA | FT | FTA | REB | PF | PTS |
|----|-----|----|-----|-----|----|-----|
| 12 | 23 | 12 | 20 | 19 | 1 | 36 |

# THE RESULT

Walker played 38 of the 40 minutes in the game against Kansas. He finished with a career-high 36 points and 19 rebounds. Danny Manning scored 30 points and pulled down 11 rebounds. Ed Davender added 20 points for the Wildcats, and Troy McKinley chipped in 12 points. Kentucky finished with an 11-7 record in the SEC and limped into the NCAAs—which had expanded to 64 teams—with a 16-12 mark.

Walker carried the team that season, averaging 22.9 points and 10.2 rebounds per game. "I think we got into the NCAA tournament because we were Kentucky," Walker says.

Still, the team earned a 12 seed and faced fifth-seeded Washington in the first round. The Wildcats won a 66-58 upset before facing fourth-seeded UNLV for a spot in the Sweet Sixteen. Kentucky recorded its second consecutive upset, 64-61, and prepared for a face-off with No. 1 seed St. John's.

The St. John's game was held in Denver. Leading up to game day, Hall led his players through a practice at nearby Regis College—where he had his first head-coaching job.

"I remember him saying something like, 'Wouldn't it be funny if my college career ended where it started?'" Ledford said. "Later that day one of Joe's buddies came up to me and told me that if the team lost that night, Joe was going to announce his resignation on the postgame show."

Lou Carnesecca's team, led by All-American Chris Mullin, proved to be too much for the Wildcats to handle, and Joe B. Hall's coaching career ended with an 86-70 defeat. After the game, Hall took longer than usual to walk out for his postgame radio show. He then read a brief statement saying he had decided to retire.

"All of us players were waiting on the team bus," Walker says. "It was taking coach longer than normal to come out. We'd heard rumors, but we didn't know what had happened."

# AFTER BLUE

Walker finished his career at Kentucky with 2,080 points—second all-time in UK history to Dan Issel's 2,138—and was an All-American in 1985 and 1986.

He was drafted No. 5 overall in the first round of the NBA Draft by the New York Knicks and later played for Rick Pitino. In 1989, Walker was scheduled to compete in the NBA's annual dunk contest. Three days before the event, Walker's father, Jerome, died of a stroke, but his mother told him to compete anyway.

"I had a lot of motivation to go out there and win," Walker says. And he did win, defeating Clyde Drexler for the title. "I felt like my Dad was out there helping me," he says.

Now Walker is single and lives in Lexington, working for radio and television stations. He also works for Kentucky Sports History, a company that uses the school's sports history to promote literacy throughout the state.

He still looks back on the Kansas game as the most important in his career. "I had a lot of big games," he says. "But that was the one that I will always remember."

# CHAPTER 14

# JOHN PELPHREY

Like countless other Kentucky kids, John and Jerry Pelphrey played basketball in the driveway of their childhood home using a makeshift basketball hoop. The two boys used to rush to chase down a loose ball, fearing that it would roll into the street and be run over by oncoming traffic.

Eventually, the games moved from the backyard to the high school gym, where Mr. and Mrs. Pelphrey worked as teachers. The gym was always open. And it was in that gym that John Pelphrey first made his name, leading his Paintsville team to three consecutive high school Sweet Sixteens. By the time he was a senior in 1987, John was named the state's best player—Mr. Basketball.

Pelphrey was a talented player who, at 6-foot-7, could step outside to hit the three. His ball handling was impressive enough for him to deftly drop passes off the break or reverse the ball outside to open shooters for assists. And his height meant he could also work inside, grabbing rebounds and seeing over defenders.

But he was slow, and he wasn't particularly strong. Pelphrey made up for those holes in his game by being cerebral. It's those same smarts that would later earn him a coaching position in the SEC.

As a player, there was always only one team for him. Since his backyard basketball days, he dreamt of playing for Kentucky. And coach Eddie Sutton agreed Pelphrey was worth the risk. John Pelphrey was going to wear blue.

# THE SETTING

Pelphrey joined fellow Kentuckian Deron Feldhaus—a Maysville native—as a redshirt for his freshman season. From the bench they watched as Kentucky raced to the Sweet Sixteen. And then the bottom fell out. NCAA sanctions and the ensuing player defections left Kentucky's team depleted. There would be no postseason play for two seasons. However, Pelphrey, along with Feldhaus and Manchester native Richie Farmer, decided to stay.

"Growing up, I always wanted to play for Kentucky," Pelphrey says. "To be there when the school needed us, we couldn't leave."

The first season was the worst, with a 13-19 record and the loss of their coach. Enter Rick Pitino: a new coach with a new attitude.

"They wanted to build Rome back up, and they stayed to do it," Rick Pitino said in his book, *Full-Court Pressure*. "They were central to what we accomplished. John was a great leader."

It all started in 1989. During Rick Pitino's first practice, Kentucky's players may have secretly wished they had left. Ray "Rock" Oliver was hired away from Pittsburgh to be Kentucky's strength and conditioning coach. Pitino said he needed a strong conditioning coach to develop the players into the kinds of athletes who could play his running, pressing style of offense and defense. For six weeks, according to Pitino, the Wildcats endured Rock's boot camp—running, sprinting, and weightlifting.

"Rock would have made a great drill instructor," Pitino wrote.

Rock required athletes to run two miles in 12 minutes. After weeks of trying, some players just could not make the time. Farmer, who came into the preseason camp at 191 pounds—20 pounds overweight—struggled, as did Pelphrey. The players had one last chance to make the time.

"John, if you belong to a church, say a prayer," Oliver said, as Pelphrey crossed the line. "You just made it. Your time was 12:00." Then Farmer crossed the line. "Richie," Oliver said, "12:01." Oliver later admitted he was not even keeping the real time, Pitino said. "He had broken all the stop watches in frustration."

Pitino knew his ragtag group, which featured just eight players,

---

John Pelphrey became UK's emotional leader during their magical run back to prominence.

would need some help if they were going to compete. The answer lay at the three-point line. "We needed a gimmick during the first season, and the three-point offense was just what the doctor ordered," Pitino wrote.

In their first games, Kentucky put up threes in record numbers. They took 53 in a 116-113 overtime loss to Southwest Louisiana, and they made 21 in a 121-110 loss to North Carolina. It became obvious that because of the team's great shooters, they could always stay in a game.

Senior guard Derrick Miller led the Wildcats with a 19 points-per-game average, and junior center Reggie Hanson added 16 points per game. Point guard Sean Woods directed the team, and Pelphrey scored 13 points per game.

"A lot of teams didn't have what we had," Pelphrey says. "We were a true team, and we played so much better than people thought we could."

They hung with 14th-ranked Indiana in a 71-69 loss. They stayed close to eighth-ranked Louisville in an 86-79 defeat. And after compiling a 12-10 record and an undefeated mark at Rupp Arena, the only thing that was lacking on the team's resume was a signature win.

In the 24th game of the season, ninth-ranked LSU came to Lexington, with Shaquille O'Neal, Stanley Roberts, and Chris Jackson in tow. O'Neal was a 7-foot bruiser who could dominate on the inside, and with teammate Roberts—an athletic 7-foot center who complemented O'Neal—the two could be unstoppable in the paint.

And Chris Jackson was yet another reason to fear the Tigers. Jackson was lightning quick—a shooting guard who could dominate a game on his own, purely from the perimeter.

How could the Wildcats—with the 6-foot-7 Hanson starting at center—ever stack up against the talented LSU Tigers? In their previous meeting in Baton Rouge, LSU had won, 94-81.

Sometimes, as Pelphrey says, you just have to believe.

# THE GAME OF MY LIFE
## KENTUCKY 100, NO. 9 LSU 95
### FEBRUARY 15, 1990
### BY JOHN PELPHREY

Being from Kentucky, every day walking out into Memorial Coliseum or Rupp Arena was like a vacation. It's hard to pick just one game, but if I had to, I'd pick the game against LSU. That's the one that got it all started.

That year, for some reason, we were undefeated at home, but we couldn't win on the road. It was all about a mind-set with us, and while it didn't serve us well on the road, we were very confident at home. Our home crowd was amazing during that time, and they really energized us. We felt really good at home.

We knew the game was played on the court, and we knew that we could beat anybody with our style. It was all about a belief system that we had as a team. We knew we could do it.

But I remember they had such awesome talent. Our team would never beat theirs on paper. It really looked like we had no chance.

But we played them anyway. And we jumped out on them like we'd never really done in a game before. We were all making shots, and our press kept forcing turnovers. We got up by more than 20 [41-18 with under seven minutes to play in the first half] and things were rolling. It's hard to use your 7-footers when you're turning the ball over at half-court.

At halftime, they had cut the lead [to 12] and we all wanted to go out and keep playing. We just focused on what we had to keep doing. But none of us figured on what Chris Jackson would do. They were a great team, so they came back, mainly because of Jackson.

The feeling we had was that he couldn't beat us by himself. But I think he went for [41 points], and he was shooting out of double teams. Then he was telling the fans to stop cheering, putting his finger over his mouth for them to be quiet.

The fans didn't stop.

Our lead was too big, and we were still scoring, so they really couldn't get all the way back. But they came close. I remember Derrick [Miller] and Deron [Feldhaus] had great games [53 points between the two of them], and that helped overcome Jackson's game. He put on a really amazing performance. But Richie ended up hitting some big free throws as we held them off [Farmer made six in the final minute].

But when it was over, we didn't have any excess celebration. Even though we were down as a team at that time, we still had pride. There were still expectations, and we were still Kentucky. We didn't want to act like it was the first time we'd done something like that. We wanted to act like we expected it to happen.

But I tell you what—there was a lot of excitement, because beating that team was a great accomplishment.

**Statline:**

| MIN | FG | FGA | FT | FTA | REB | A | S | B | PTS |
|-----|-----|-----|-----|-----|-----|-----|-----|-----|-----|
| 32 | 3 | 10 | 3 | 5 | 5 | 2 | 7 | 1 | 10 |

# THE RESULT

When it was over, Richie Farmer raised his index finger. Kentucky had pulled off the upset, 100-95. "That was the signal for the crowd to finally release the emotion that had lifted and carried this team all night, beginning with the pregame warm-ups," wrote the *Lexington Herald-Leader's* Billy Reed. "The ensuing roar, an explosion of joy, was the ultimate tribute to this team."

Pelphrey finished with 10 points, as did Farmer, and Hanson scored 11 points, while also grabbing 12 rebounds and dishing six assists. Woods scored 12 points and also had seven assists.

"My esteem for this team can go no higher," Pitino told the *Herald-Leader.* "This is an amazing bunch of guys."

Afterward, Pitino told the team the LSU game was their NCAA Tournament. And he lavished Jackson with praise. "I've never seen a guy have a game like that," Pitino told the *Herald-Leader,* "except maybe for Michael Jordan one night in the NBA."

But Jackson could not overshadow what was a magnificent game for the Kentucky team. "They play smart, they play hard, they create chaos, and they never quit," Reed wrote. "Mostly, they dare to dream."

The game, which would go down as one of the most memorable victories in Wildcats history, was not televised due to the team's NCAA probation.

The team would go on to a 14-14 record, causing some local sports writers to dub Pitino a "miracle worker." But it was the players who made the baskets and put in the work. "It was all about believing you could do it, and working hard," Pelphrey says.

\* \* \*

In Pelphrey's junior season, the Wildcats received help from star recruit Jamal Mashburn, and immediately, the Wildcats went 22-6 and finished No. 1 in the SEC. In just two seasons, Kentucky was back.

But they were again unable to participate in the NCAA

Tournament. "That was tough," Pelphrey says. "But we were still the best in the league."

As a senior, Pelphrey became the team's emotional leader, and the 1992 Wildcats were a force. With a record of 29-7, Kentucky showed how far they had come by winning the SEC Tournament and taking No. 1 Duke to the brink before falling in overtime, 104-103. Pelphrey would just miss appearing in the Final Four. "That Duke game was a hard, hard way to end your career," he says.

# AFTER BLUE

The greatest honor was reserved for later. At the team's post-game ceremony, Pelphrey, Woods, Feldhaus, and Farmer had their jerseys hung in Rupp Arena. "I could've never imagined it, really," Pelphrey says.

Their team was called The Unforgettables.

On road trips, sometimes Pelphrey would jump in the front seat of the team bus and announce how he would someday be the coach at Kentucky. And maybe someday he will.

After stints as an assistant with Oklahoma State, Marshall, and Florida [both with former Kentucky assistant Billy Donovan], Pelphrey was named head coach at South Alabama, where he led the team to the Sun Belt Conference Tournament title and a spot in the 2006 NCAA Tournament. In 2007, he was named head coach at Arkansas. But he will always be known as an Unforgettable.

Now, he tells his own teams about what can happen if they believe. "That team and that game will always stay with me," he says of the LSU win. "It's something I will always use to motivate my own players."

# CHAPTER 15

# REGGIE HANSON

Technically, Reggie Hanson was not a Kentucky kid. Born in Charlotte, North Carolina, Hanson's family moved to Somerset, Kentucky, when he was young. But when he discovered basketball, he became ingrained in the Kentucky tradition.

"Every kid in Kentucky grows up wanting to be a Wildcat," he says. "If you get that chance, you take it."

Hanson, a versatile big man, became a standout player at Pulaski County, leading his high school squad to a state title in 1986. Even though he wasn't a native Kentuckian, he knew enough about Kentucky and basketball to know where he wanted to go to college.

"It was always Kentucky," he says.

## THE SETTING

Hanson sat out during his freshman season for academic reasons, but he became a solid contributor in coach Eddie Sutton's final year, averaging more than nine points per game. That, of course, is when everything changed in Kentucky basketball. A scandal, a new coach, and a new athletic director amounted to a new environment at UK.

Hanson could've transferred and played that season, along with athletic guard Derrick Miller. But both players stayed at UK. "I made a commitment," Hanson says. "A lot of SEC and ACC schools came calling, where Derrick and I could've played immediately, but we wanted to stay and help bring Kentucky back."

Hanson and Miller, along with Richie Farmer, Deron Feldhaus, John Pelphrey, Sean Woods, and Jeff Brassow, would constitute the core of the team that would lead Kentucky back to prominence. But no one knew that at the time.

During Rick Pitino's first press conference, he promised fans that the team would win—and win "right away." Radio broadcaster Cawood Ledford said it would be a "miracle" if the team won ten games.

"In Rick's very first year they were predicting us to win five or six games," Hanson says. "No one really knew what to expect. But after we'd been through some of Rick's practices, we knew there was a whole new attitude."

\* \* \*

Hanson would later use both Pitino's, as well as coach Tubby Smith's teachings when he became an assistant coach for the Big Blue in 2000. Hanson decided on two favorite games—one as a player, another as an assistant—that stand out in his memory.

In 1990, Hanson was a junior at Kentucky, playing in Pitino's first season as head coach. The Wildcats had already reeled off 12 victories, far more than some predicted. But then came ninth-ranked LSU, with future pros Shaquille O'Neal, Stanley Roberts, and Chris Jackson. It would become the signature victory of the early Pitino era.

In 2003, Hanson had been a UK assistant coach for three seasons. Many felt that the power in the SEC was shifting to the Florida Gators, who had recently earned the school's first-ever No. 1 ranking. But the Gators were in for a surprise.

Reggie Hanson played and coached at Kentucky, and helped recruit the nation's No.1 class to the school in 2004.

# THE GAMES OF MY LIFE
## AS A PLAYER:
### KENTUCKY 100, NO. 9 LSU 95
### FEBRUARY 15,1990
## AS AN ASSISTANT COACH:
### NO. 6 KENTUCKY 70, NO. 1 FLORIDA 55
### FEBRUARY 4, 2003
**BY REGGIE HANSON**

As a player, [my favorite game] would have to be the upset over LSU. We were up late in that game, and we just took over. And we were able to hit free throws down the stretch to win it. It was one of the biggest upsets ever for Kentucky. Even though it was in Coach Pitino's first year, Coach said it was going to be the biggest win we'd ever have. He was right. It was huge for the state of Kentucky and huge for us.

I loved competing against the best, and it didn't get any better than Shaquille O'Neal and that LSU team. We knew how it looked to everyone else on the outside—it looked like we couldn't win. But we had a way, and our coach helped us find the way.

Rick was a great motivator, and he started the first day of what he called our "boot camp" by thanking those of us who stayed. He thanked me, and he thanked Derrick Miller, and he thanked Richie Farmer, John Pelphrey, Deron Feldhaus, Sean Woods, and Jeff Brassow. Then we all went through hell physically and mentally. That's what prepared us for that game.

The LSU game had to be later in the season for us to really be competitive, because it took us until then to realize how good we could be and how disruptive we could make life for other teams.

We had lost in our first game against LSU by 13, but that was in Baton Rouge. A big difference in that game and our second game with them was our crowd—it was unbelievable. The game wasn't televised because we were on probation, but we still had our 23,000 [fans] in the crowd for us. It was such a great confidence boost to have them cheering for us. Kentucky fans don't take a day off—they live and die with every win and loss.

When we came out hitting almost every shot, we gained our confidence. Just the fact that we were in the game after 10 minutes gave us a lot of confidence. But we were able to do things like that because we really liked each other, and that enabled us to play so well. We believed we could beat anyone at anytime.

And of course, I remember Chris Jackson and his unbelievable game. I remember him hitting all those shots in the second half and putting his finger to his mouth, telling the crowd to be quiet.

We didn't do things like that. We came to play. And we won.

**Statline:**

| MIN | FG | FGA | 3FG | 3FTA | REB | A | PTS |
|-----|----|----|----|----|----|----|----|
| 40 | 4 | 12 | 1 | 3 | 12 | 6 | 11 |

\* \* \*

As an assistant [coach], I'd have to say the most exciting game I was a part of was when we beat No. 1 Florida in Rupp [Arena] in 2003. Florida came in, and they'd just become No. 1 in the country. But that game was over just after it began. You could see it in the Florida players' faces. They just gave up—you could tell it was over.

That was a pretty talented Kentucky team, with Marquis Estill, Keith Bogans, Gerald Fitch, and others. They were completely professional and came out and just got the job done. That game was laughable, though. But it's the only time I've ever heard a crowd as loud as that LSU game I played in.

\* \* \*

Both were two totally different games. Against Florida, we were definitely a top 25 team, and we would prove how good we were as the season went on. Against LSU, we were not a ranked club, and we were undermanned.

The only similarity: both teams had a perceived lack of talent. No one outside of the players and coaches knew how talented either of those teams was. But each team had some players who could play. And I was happy to be a part of both teams.

# THE RESULT

"Without a doubt, we definitely set the foundation for the years to come," Hanson says. "We were a team that people still don't talk that much about. We went 14-14 when a lot of people thought we'd have a losing season. We set the foundation for the future."

Hanson scored 11 points and added 12 rebounds and six assists. In Hanson's senior season, a 6-foot-9 freshman named Jamal

Mashburn joined the roster, and the team became one of the best in the country. The Wildcats went 22-6, 14-4 in the league, and finished ranked No. 9 in the nation. Both Hanson and Pelphrey led the way in scoring with averages of 14.4 points per game. The team finished with the best record in the SEC, and for that, they were given special rings.

Hanson's career fell just short of the NCAA Tournament, as the team was removed from probation the following season.

# AFTER BLUE

"It's rare a person can play here and then coach here," Hanson says. "It's rare and special." After leaving Kentucky, Hanson relocated to Japan, where he played professionally for eight seasons.

In 1998, Pitino—the head coach of the Boston Celtics at the time—called Hanson and invited him to the NBA. For two months of one season, Hanson was on an NBA roster. He appeared in eight games. Then he returned to Japan for two more seasons before coming back to Kentucky as an assistant coach. "Coaching was something I was always interested in," he says.

From 2000 to 2002, Hanson helped coach stars like Tayshaun Prince and Keith Bogans. But those Kentucky teams never reached their potential in the NCAA Tournament.

Then, in 2003, Keith Bogans led a talented UK squad that reeled off 26 straight victories—including the smearing of No. 1 Florida—en route to a birth in the NCAA regional finals. Only a superhuman triple-double effort by Marquette star Dwyane Wade, as well as an ankle injury sustained by Bogans, kept the Wildcats from the Final Four.

Now Hanson is ready to participate in more big games—but as an assistant coach at South Florida. He still has the ring he received in 1991—the season Kentucky posted the best record in the SEC. And he's proud of all of his years as a Wildcat.

"When I made a commitment to come here, I felt it was my duty to stay," he says. "When you start something, you don't just quit when you see a detour."

# CHAPTER 16

# RICHIE FARMER

The legend of Richie Farmer was in full bloom long before he ever wore Kentucky blue. In the early 1980s, Farmer's star began to rise in tiny Manchester, nestled in the eastern Kentucky mountains of Clay County, where he led Clay County High to the state's Sweet Sixteen basketball tournament as an eighth grader.

Farmer guided his team to the tournament the next four years as well, becoming the only player in Kentucky high school history to appear in five consecutive Sweet Sixteens.

The beauty of the tournament has always been that teams from all of Kentucky's 16 regions, no matter how big or small, can compete to win the state's lone basketball title. For decades, players have made their reputations in the state tournament.

During the mid- and late 1980s, two high schools established themselves as powers on opposing sides of the Bluegrass state; and two legendary high school players carved their places in Kentucky basketball history.

To the east, Richie Farmer, with his shooting touch and toughness, made Clay County a force in the tournament. Farmer overcame a lack of size by pouring in jumpers and using his quickness to evade defenders. When fouled, he was nearly automatic from the free-throw line.

To the west, in the big city of Louisville, Allan Houston was leading Ballard High School on a similar course. At 6-foot-4, Houston was a legitimate NBA prospect, with size, a soft jump shot from three-point range, and the ability to drive to the basket. He was an explosive scorer and could take over a game at will.

Different in so many ways, the two players would grow accustomed to seeing one another in high school and in college.

\* \* \*

After racing to the Sweet Sixteen in 1983 and 1984, Clay County—led by sophomore Richie Farmer—advanced to the coveted state championship game in 1985, at which point they fell to Hopkinsville, 65-64.

As a junior, Farmer thirsted for the championship. Again, Clay County reached the title game. This time, they faced Ballard High and talented sophomore Allan Houston. After an overtime and 18 points from Farmer, Clay County claimed the title, 76-73.

Farmer's senior season almost had a storybook ending. He led his defending state champions to his record fifth state tournament appearance, in which they advanced to a third consecutive championship game.

Again, Houston and Ballard stood in Clay County's way. Farmer did all that he could, pouring in a record 51 points in the title game. But Ballard was too much to handle, and Houston finally earned his state title, 88-79. Farmer won the state's Mr. Basketball award. Houston would succeed him the following year.

"We had some intense basketball games in high school," Farmer says of his duels with Houston. "He was an extremely talented player, and we had a devil of a time every time we had to play them."

In high school, Farmer made it known that he intended to play for Kentucky—if then-coach Eddie Sutton would have him. In Louisville, coach Denny Crum expressed interest in Farmer, as did LSU coach Dale Brown.

"I basically made it known I wanted to go to UK," Farmer says. "But LSU still came after me pretty hard. Dale Brown came to my house and basically told me what he expected. He said it would be great to have a backcourt of Chris Jackson and Richie Farmer. I told him I appreciated his honesty, but that I'd grown up in Kentucky. I said that if Kentucky offered me a scholarship, that's where I was going to go."

---

Richie Farmer was already a Kentucky basketball legend before he ever put on a Wildcat uniform.

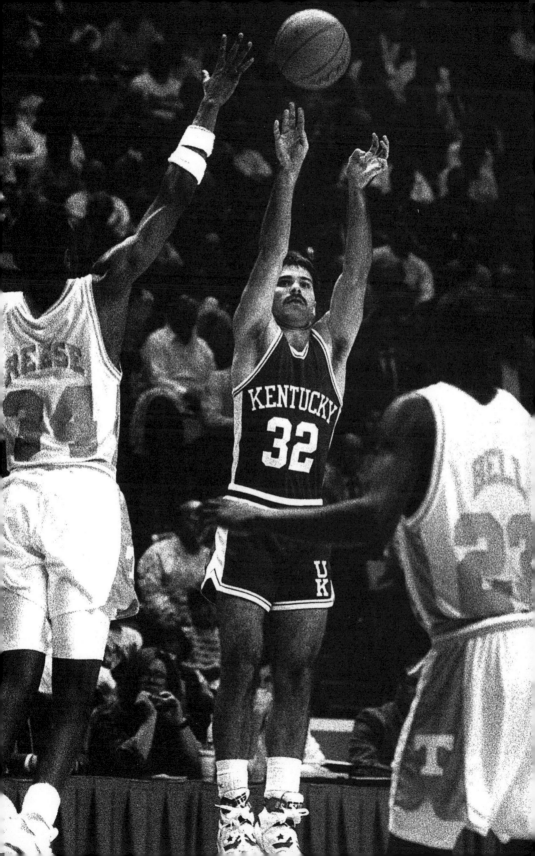

And in 1988, Farmer signed to play with the Wildcats. Even Farmer's press conference to announce his commitment to the Wildcats became legendary.

But during the very same week, an Emery freight package broke open in Los Angeles. Inside was $1,000, earmarked for UK recruit Chris Mills. After learning of the incident, the media asked Farmer if he was reconsidering his decision. But the Clay County guard never hesitated. He was still going to UK, and he doubted anything would come of the situation.

It was widely thought that Houston—who was one of the top high school prospects in the nation by then—would attend Louisville, where his father, Wade, was an assistant coach.

But the situation changed after Wade Houston accepted the head coaching position at Tennessee. Houston, the best basketball player in the state of Kentucky in 1989, would instead become a Tennessee Volunteer. He would face Farmer at least twice a season.

# THE SETTING

In his freshman season, Farmer hit a game-winning three point shot against Ole Miss. But that may have been the best moment of the year.

During university and NCAA investigations, Kentucky suffered through a 13-19 season—the school's first losing campaign in 61 years. More violations were uncovered, including a questionable college entrance exam score for high school star Eric Manuel. After that season, Sutton was gone, as was the school's athletic director. The punishment was severe: a two-year ban from the NCAA Tournament, no television appearances, and a reduction in scholarships.

The most talented players transferred. But Farmer remained devoted to the UK, as did fellow Kentuckians Deron Feldhaus, John Pelphrey, and Reggie Hanson, along with sharpshooter Derrick Miller and point guard Sean Woods (who hailed from Indiana, although he had family in Lexington).

"We were committed to Kentucky," Farmer says. Farmer and his fellow Wildcats would become a part of one of the most beloved teams in Kentucky history.

\* \* \*

The team flourished under the direction of Rick Pitino during Farmer's sophomore year. They used their up-tempo style and frenetic defense to post a 14-14 record, including a split with Tennessee, which featured the precocious freshman Allan Houston.

By the time Farmer was a junior, Kentucky was back on top in the SEC. Farmer averaged 10 points per game for the 22-6 Wildcats. And with the addition of talented freshman Jamal Mashburn, Kentucky finished with the best record in the SEC at 14-4 and scored two more victories over Tennessee. But with probation banning postseason play, Farmer, Feldhaus, Pelphrey, and Woods would have to wait until their senior year for a taste of the NCAA Tournament.

In 1992, the world knew Kentucky basketball was back. It was a magical senior season for Farmer and the team. They had returned to the nation's top ten rankings. They were again on the hunt for the conference championship. The memories of probation were officially behind them.

But among the team's six losses that season was a 107-85 spanking at the hands of Houston and Tennessee. Allan Houston scored 36 points. "But we were our own worst enemy," Pitino said in his book, *Full-Court Pressure*. The Wildcats made just six of 32 three-pointers and committed 24 turnovers. They were called for a school-record 41 fouls, and five players fouled out. Richie Farmer and the Wildcats seniors would have to avenge the humiliating loss on Senior Day.

\* \* \*

"For a kid growing up in Kentucky, wearing that blue and white, playing in Rupp Arena in front of 24,000 fans every night—when you know that's going to be your last night, you have a lot of thoughts going through your head when you step out on to that floor," Farmer says. "Then they start playing 'My Old Kentucky Home,' and it tugs on your heartstrings."

In 1978, NBC broadcasted Kentucky's Senior Day ceremony, and it left the journalists speechless. "[It] is one of the grand traditions in college basketball," Pitino said in his book. But this day was even more special. The seniors who had endured Kentucky's trying times were leaving. And so was Cawood Ledford, Kentucky's legendary radio announcer, who planned to retire at the end of the year.

The team was finally off of probation, and fans were ready for another postseason run. They were given rally towels to wave and cheer. Scalpers were getting a reported $400 per ticket for the game. And to cap it off, Hollywood director Spike Lee was invited to the game by Pitino while Lee was in the area promoting a new movie. It made for an unforgettable scene.

And it seemed appropriate that Farmer would conclude his college career in the same manner as he had ended his high school basketball days—against his old rival, Allan Houston and the Tennessee Volunteers.

# THE GAME OF MY LIFE
## NO. 10 KENTUCKY 99, TENNESSEE 88
### MARCH 7, 1992
#### BY RICHIE FARMER

All the pageantry and the ceremony of Senior Day—before the game I had a few tears in my eyes. My family was there, and the other seniors' families were all there. Then they played "My Old Kentucky Home," and that's when it got really hard to hold all the emotion back. I didn't want to lose focus.

People always ask me if I ever got nervous before a game. Well, I always had a feeling, but I think that feeling was just me thinking about what I wanted to do. That's what I was trying to do on Senior Day.

When the ceremony was over, we got it together and went to half court, where the Tennessee captains were. We never talked a lot of trash at all. We just met there on the court and talked friendly for a second. We wished each other luck, and after that, it was business as usual. It was always good to go against Allan. It seemed fitting that after I played my last high school game against him, I was playing my last college game at Rupp against him, too.

If I remember right, I came out on fire. I ended up getting us off to a good start by scoring ten straight points in the early part of the game, and we got an early lead. We were so excited because it was such a special day. We really had to settle down a little. But once we came out of the gate, we started feeling good.

I hit some threes, and we got into our rhythm. Mash was having his way. Then Sean ended up getting hit, and he hit his man [Tennessee guard Jay Price] back. Both got ejected. How about that? Sean got ejected from a Senior Day game. It was a shame, too, because he was playing really well.

112

Then we struggled a little. Travis Ford, who was a little hurt, and I had to fill in at the point guard spot, and they came back on us; we were down at half [47-46]. At the half, we talked about knowing what we had to do. None of us wanted to lose on Senior Day. It was a good thing we had Mash, too.

It was our game to push teams so hard that we won the game in the end, and that's what we did. With [six minutes] to go, we went on a big run [15-3] to blow open a close game. I hit some free throws and a layup and made a steal during the run. We ended up winning it going away, but the game was closer than it looked.

And that meant the most to all of us. Afterward, there was just jubilation because we were so satisfied about the season we'd had and the win. It all meant so much to us because we were from Kentucky, and we'd really wanted to see Kentucky basketball come back to being the best.

We all got the opportunity to live the dream.

## Statline:

| FG | FGA | 3FG | 3FGA | FT | FTA | A | PTS |
|----|-----|-----|------|----|-----|---|-----|
| 5  | 7   | 2   | 3    | 3  | 3   | 4 | 15  |

# THE RESULT

Kentucky basketball was definitely back. The Wildcats finished the regular season 22-6. Farmer scored 15 points against Tennessee and defeated Allan Houston on Senior Day.

Houston scored 23 points in the losing effort, while Mashburn scored 30 points and grabbed 10 rebounds. Pelphrey added nine points and seven assists, while Feldhaus scored 13 points. Woods finished with six assists in just 12 minutes.

Farmer was also an integral part of a postgame ceremony honoring Ledford's last home broadcast. When Richie was just eight years old, he met the legendary broadcaster while Ledford was shopping in a Hazard clothing store. The two had formed a special bond when Farmer came to UK. Farmer was chosen to represent the players during the goodbye ceremony.

"When I was growing up in eastern Kentucky, I used to listen to Cawood, and he was Kentucky basketball," Farmer said that day. "Kids growing up all have their heroes. Some are basketball players, wrestlers, and country music singers. Mine was Cawood Ledford.

And now that I've gotten to know him after four years at Kentucky, he's still my hero."

The crowd, which had stayed for the event, joined in as the cheerleaders, players, and staff sang one last rendition of "My Old Kentucky Home."

\* \* \*

The Wildcats went on to win the SEC Tournament, led by Mashburn, the tournament's MVP. "We had a great tournament coach," Farmer says. "And as a team, we were seniors, and we wanted to keep going as far as we could. We knew we'd never get to do this again."

After earning a No. 2 seed in the NCAA Tournament, Kentucky's dream season ended at the hands of the Duke Blue Devils, 104-103, in overtime in the regional finals. Farmer missed his opportunity to play in the Final Four.

"But we gave them the best game we could have," he says. "Together, our team accomplished what a lot of people said was not possible."

At the team's banquet following the end of the season, Farmer, Feldhaus, Pelphrey, and Woods received Kentucky's ultimate honor: Their jerseys were hung from Rupp Arena's rafters. "An incredible feeling," Farmer says.

And because of their amazing connection to Kentucky fans, the team earned a nickname to be remembered alongside the Fabulous Five, the Fiddling Five, and Rupp's Runts. Farmer's senior season squad would forever be known as The Unforgettables.

# AFTER BLUE

After leaving Kentucky, Farmer went into the insurance business in his hometown of Manchester. But many across the state always said Farmer could use his popularity to run for political office.

And he did. In 2003, Richie ran for the state's Commissioner of Agriculture. After all, what better job could there be for a man named Farmer?

The Wildcats legend knows his basketball celebrity helped his cause. "Anybody that grows up in Kentucky and plays basketball at Kentucky is certainly going to have opportunities," he says. "You just have to take advantage of them."

Now Farmer works in Frankfort, and he still takes his three sons to the Sweet Sixteen tournament. To this day, he remains friends with Allan Houston, who is now a retired NBA player and a basketball analyst for ESPN. But Farmer will always be remembered as one of The Unforgettables.

"Our team certainly knew that if you took us and the opposing team, and you lined us up on paper, we weren't going to beat anybody," Farmer says. "But we knew we had to play for 40 minutes, because of the talent we had, and we really thought we could beat anybody. It was a classic case of the whole being greater than the sum of the parts. Together, we were a great college basketball team, because we loved each other and we were willing to do anything to get it done.

"I wouldn't trade my life for anybody's in the world," he says. "I just want to say thanks to all the fans."

# CHAPTER 17

# JAMAL MASHBURN

As a young New Yorker, Jamal Mashburn watched businessmen board the subway in the Bronx, briefcases in hand. "Someday," he thought, "I'll carry a briefcase, too." But after years of playing basketball, Mashburn left the streets of New York.

Mashburn honed his basketball skills in pickup games. He eventually made his way to Cardinal Hayes High School where he became a prep star and developed into one of the most versatile high school big men in the nation—someone who could step out and hit a jumper and step inside to use strength and skill in the paint. He earned Mr. Basketball honors in the state of New York. And Kentucky was the furthest thing from his mind.

"I was a Syracuse fan," he says. "Coming from New York, Syracuse was the biggest thing at that time. Everyone in New York loves the Big East, so it was natural." But he also loved Wake Forest; and he knew he would attend either Wake Forest or Syracuse. Many other colleges knew this, too, and accepted it as fact.

It only took a couple of college visits to change his mind. At Wake Forest, he immediately felt uncomfortable in such a small environment. At Syracuse, his dream to play for the Orangemen waned—the team seemed a bit crowded. "They had a lot of talent at that time," Mashburn says of Syracuse. "I looked at their team, and they had a lot of All-Americans. I wondered where I would fit in."

So he began speaking to fellow New Yorker Rick Pitino, who encouraged him to consider the University of Kentucky.

"Everyone knows Coach Pitino is a good salesman," Mashburn says. "But he was also very honest with me. He told me exactly how difficult the situation could be. But he also said how rewarding it could be."

\* \* \*

According to Mashburn, the team at Cardinal Hayes was cohesive: No infighting and no agendas. "I'm not sure if there was one other player on our team who went to a Division I school," he says. "So that season was their big moment. They gave everything they had to their school because it was the biggest thing they could hope for." And that team won a state championship.

Mashburn sensed the same spirit on a visit to Kentucky's campus. "Those guys reminded me of my high school teammates, in the way they wanted so much to win for their team, and even their state," he says of the UK team. "I knew that Coach Pitino—a New York guy who coached the Knicks and a former Big East coach—could make me a better player. I didn't know then if I was good enough to make it to the NBA. But I knew *he* knew what it took, and he could help me.

"He told me that I could help bring UK basketball back to the way it used to be," he says. "I wanted to be a part of that."

# THE SETTING

Mashburn became the single most important recruit for Pitino's rebuilding project. The *Parade* All-American forward knew Kentucky still had a year to serve on its three-year ban from the NCAA Tournament. There would be no postseason play after Mashburn's freshman season.

"I didn't feel too bad about that," Mashburn says. "It wasn't a big factor in making my decision. I looked at it as me learning my way, serving an apprenticeship for a year before going to the tournament."

"Everybody recognized Jamal's ability," Pitino said in his book *Full-Court Pressure,* "they just questioned whether he would work hard."

In his first conditioning session with the Wildcats, Mashburn was

Jamal Mashburn was the first heralded recruit to commit to the Kentucky program while the Wildcats were on probation.

asked to run a mile by strength coach Rock Oliver. "I didn't know what conditioning was," Mashburn says. "I thought I was in shape. They told us to run a mile, and I thought a mile was a distance you traveled in a car."

Mashburn struggled so much with preseason conditioning that he admits to having thoughts of quitting basketball. "They pushed you to the point where you thought you couldn't take it anymore," he says.

During a preseason practice, Mashburn reached a breaking point. He fell behind in one of the many mandatory team running drills. His savior came from the mountains of eastern Kentucky.

"Richie Farmer stayed back with me, to encourage me to keep going," Mashburn says. "He helped me and told me I could do it. It was the beginning of the relationship I would have with that team. And it helped me realize more of where the other players came from."

It took the six-foot guard from Manchester—the player who achieved a cult-like following in high school but only reluctantly drew a scholarship offer from Kentucky—to help the 6-foot-8 prep All-American from the Bronx survive a Kentucky practice.

"We became dear friends after that," Mashburn says.

* * *

Mashburn averaged nearly 13 points as a freshman starter, setting a UK record for a single-game mark by a freshman with 31 points against Georgia. The team exceeded all expectations with a 22-6 record and a 14-4 mark in conference—the best in the league. But the Wildcats were still ineligible for postseason play.

Along the way, Mashburn grew closer to his teammates. He bonded with Paintsville native John Pelphrey when the two drove to Cincinnati to see controversial comedian Andrew Dice Clay. "That's how we got to know each other," he says. "Even though we were from different places, we still had things in common. That's how it was with everybody on our team. We all liked one another. We all got along."

As a sophomore, Mashburn averaged 21.3 points and 7.8 rebounds on a team that, according to many in the media, was among the top ten in America.

"All that season, we felt like we had something special," Mashburn says. "We felt like something special was going to happen. It took me back to high school, when I looked at my teammates, and

I knew this was their moment. Many weren't going into the NBA. This was their career. I wanted to do something for them."

At the end of the 1991-92 regular season, Kentucky was 23-6 and ranked No. 10 in the nation. Included in the season were impressive wins over Indiana, Louisville, and a 107-83 thrashing of Alabama. But among the losses was a 74-53 drubbing at the hands of Shaquille O'Neal and LSU. When the conference tournament began in Birmingham, Alabama, many thought Kentucky, LSU, Alabama, and sixth-ranked Arkansas were the favorites. It was the Wildcats' first taste of postseason play during the Pitino era.

The tournament began well. Kentucky defeated Vanderbilt 73-57 to force a rematch with LSU sans Shaquille O'Neal, who was suspended for fighting in the Tigers' first-round game against Tennessee. Kentucky won a hard-fought game, 80-74. On the other side of the bracket, Alabama upset Arkansas, sinking a three-pointer with a second remaining, to set up the UK/Alabama title game.

In their post-probation NCAA Tournament debut, Kentucky was playing for a championship. "I told Mash before the game that he needed to be the best player on the floor," Pitino wrote. "[He] played like the best player in the country."

# THE GAME OF MY LIFE
## NO. 9 KENTUCKY 80, NO. 17 ALABAMA 54
### MARCH 15, 1992
#### BY JAMAL MASHBURN

I couldn't give the seniors on that team, the ones I had gotten so close to, anything that you had to buy. I didn't have any money, so I couldn't go out and buy anything. But I knew I could give them a conference championship.

That time was a defining period for me, as a player and a person. As a team, we really came together so well. We were playing great basketball, and the only way I could repay those guys was to send them out as champions.

I knew the type of talent I had, but I always identified with the underdog. And I always still felt that mentality. We got a little lucky in the SEC Tournament when Shaq was suspended for our game. I mean, who wants to play him, right? But we still had to play Alabama—Robert Horry, James "Hollywood" Robinson, and Latrell Sprewell.

But we were confident going into the game, because we knew what it meant to us, to the state, and the school; and we felt like we had a good command of the system we were playing in.

In the first half, we started out slow, and I think we were down at halftime [32-29].

But before the second half, I got everyone together, and I told them that to win we had to work harder. Then we started playing like we knew we could.

When you're in the zone, like people say, and you're playing for people other than yourself, the ball comes to you. It gets easier. And everybody on that team was unselfish. At the end of the day, nobody cared what his stats were. It was all about winning, and each player was an asset.

Our whole goal was to press them until they wore out, and we did, putting together something like a [30-to-6] run on them in the second half. We knew that we could press them, even though we'd pressed three times in three days over the course of the tournament. We were physically fit and ready. And it wore them out in that second half. You could see it.

In the end, we won a championship. It reminded me of high school, when I wanted to give my teammates a state championship. I'm still so proud we were able to win the SEC like that.

## Statline:

| FG | FGA | 3FG | 3FGA | FT | FTA | REB | PF | PTS |
|----|-----|-----|------|----|-----|-----|----|-----|
| 12 | 14  | 1   | 1    | 3  | 6   | 13  | 3  | 28  |

# THE RESULT

For Alabama, Robinson scored 22 points, Horry scored 11 points, and Sprewell chipped in six points. Only two other players scored.

Mashburn finished 26-31 from the field for the three games of the tournament, grabbing 30 rebounds and snagging the SEC Tournament MVP. The team cut down the championship nets and prepared for a trip to the NCAA Tournament.

"We used that momentum," Mashburn says. "That carried over to our performances in the NCAA Tournament."

That season, Kentucky approached the brink of the Final Four before falling to No.1 Duke 104-103 in overtime of the regional finals. It was a heartbreaking way for the seniors to leave UK basketball; but, nevertheless, they showed the world that Kentucky basketball was back.

"I love to think about that SEC Tournament," Mashburn says. "It was so important for us to win. We were so excited then. I think it doesn't matter who we played in those games—we could've played the L.A. Lakers and we still would have won."

Mashburn played one more season for the Big Blue. He averaged 21 points and 8.3 rebounds as a junior, earning consensus All-America honors and the SEC Player of the Year award. He led his team to wins over Indiana, Louisville, LSU, Arkansas, Utah, and Wake Forest, and he scored at least 20 points in 21 of UK's 34 games that year.

He capped off a dream season for Kentucky fans with a Final Four trip in 1993. "We put Kentucky basketball back on the map," he says.

# AFTER BLUE

After his junior season, Mashburn left Kentucky for the NBA. He was drafted by the Dallas Mavericks. And after more than 10 years in the league, including one All-Star appearance and a 50-point game, Mashburn retired from basketball in 2004.

He now owns a car dealership and serves as an analyst for ESPN's *Fast Break* television show. And now he gets to carry that briefcase he dreamt about as a child. "I enjoy basketball, but my dream was to carry the briefcase," he says. "I have an entrepreneurial spirit. I want to get involved in more things."

Mashburn says he would still root for Pitino, even after he took the head coaching job with the rival Louisville Cardinals. "The way I look at it, I had some great coaches, and that relationship doesn't change," he says. "It would be wrong of me not to support them. Still, the only team I watch on television is Kentucky. I still cheer for UK first. I love Kentucky.

"I always think back to the career I had, and I remember the teammates and the practices," he says. "It wasn't necessarily the wins and the losses that we had that I remember; it was the impact we made on the history of Kentucky basketball. Coach Pitino told me that we could do something special, and we did."

---

# CHAPTER 18

# AMINU TIMBERLAKE

Six feet, nine inches tall. Lean and lanky. Aminu Timberlake of De LaSalle High School had his choice of colleges. Not surprisingly, the schools were all basketball powerhouses. Georgetown or Michigan. Indiana or DePaul. Or of course, Kentucky.

Not bad for a Chicago kid who didn't start playing the game until the eighth grade. "I was always tall—already about 6-foot-4 or 6-foot-5 in eighth grade, so I started playing," says Timberlake. "People always told me, 'I wish I had your height.'"

And after arriving at Kentucky, he became fast friends with another 6-foot-9 freshman center, Andre Riddick. But the two needed to gain weight if they wanted to play. Timberlake weighed in at a waif-like 195 pounds.

"There was an opportunity there to play with a lot of great athletes, like Jamal Mashburn, and to be a part of all that tradition," Timberlake says of his time at Kentucky. "Most of my contributions to the team were made in practice. I remember being so excited before going out on the court. And when I was playing, I would get into foul trouble because I was so excited."

He averaged 1.1 points per game his freshman season. "It was just constantly exciting, and you remember and appreciate it more and more as you get older," Timberlake says.

## THE SETTING

Duke had seized its biggest lead—12 points—and the momentum lay with the Blue Devils. Something had to be done. Rick Pitino called a timeout to regroup his Kentucky Wildcats.

For much of the 1992 NCAA East Regional final, Kentucky had hung with the mighty Blue Devils—the first-ranked defending champions. The Wildcats started the game hot, seizing a 20-12 lead on two threes by senior John Pelphrey. But Duke responded with a quick 11-2 run to reclaim control. The Blue Devils led 50-45 at the half.

Pitino was certain the Wildcats should open with a zone defense, because they couldn't defend Duke's All-America players one on one. For much of the game, the zone allowed the Wildcats to stay close. But now the contest was getting away from them.

During the timeout, Pitino called for all-out man-to-man defense, thinking the Wildcats' full-court pressure was wearing down the Blue Devils. "He said it was our time," Timberlake remembers. "He said we were going to win."

Pitino looked like a prophet. Jamal Mashburn converted two consecutive steals by senior Deron Feldhaus into three-pointers. Just like that, Kentucky was back in the game.

But Duke would not give up easily. The Blue Devils stretched their lead back to nine and looked to be in command—until fate intervened.

With 8:06 to go in the game, Duke's All-America center Christian Laettner went to the basket and was fouled by Timberlake, who crashed to the floor. Laettner stumbled and brought his foot down on the chest of the Kentucky player. The arena erupted.

Duke players rushed to calm Laettner. Officials called a technical foul on the Duke star. Timberlake got up, smiled, and began clapping. TV commentators debated whether or not Laettner had purposefully stepped on Timberlake. "Yeah he did," said play-by-play man Verne Lundquist.

Replays proved Lundquist correct.

"I hadn't known Laettner had stepped on him," Pitino later wrote in his book, *Full-Court Pressure.* "I turned to my assistants and asked, 'What happened?'

"If I had seen the incident, I would have gone crazy and demanded that Laettner be ejected from the game," Pitino wrote. "But I never saw the play until the news that night."

---

Aminu Timberlake will always be remembered as the victim of
Christian Laettner's stomp.

Laettner was not ejected. And ultimately he was the difference in a heart-wrenchingly close game.

When Duke guard Bobby Hurley missed an off-balance jumper at the buzzer, Kentucky and Duke were tied. Five more minutes were needed to decide which team would go to the Final Four.

Duke wanted to defend its national championship from 1991. Kentucky, fresh off a postseason ban, wanted to show the basketball world it was back on top. And when Sean Woods' 13-foot runner arched over Laettner's outstretched arm, banked off the backboard, and fell through the net with 2.1 seconds remaining, the world thought UK had won.

"We thought that was it," Timberlake said. "We thought we had it."

* * *

Afterward, the sportswriters had trouble finding words for their stories. The game was so big—too big to describe. To this day, Kentucky basketball fans remember where they were when Laettner hit The Shot.

Timberlake had more than a small part in the game. Though he played just five minutes, people would remember his name for all time—just as they would forever remember The Stomp.

For a kid from Chicago—a kid who'd towered over his peers since grade school—Timberlake never knew he'd become the target of college basketball's biggest star. The star who, upon one lapse of clear thinking, became the game's big bully.

Timberlake was a skinny center. He and his best friend Riddick helped fill in for the regular starter, Gimel Martinez. The fact that Timberlake was in at all in that stage of the game was a bit of a fluke. Foul trouble plagued Kentucky throughout the Duke game, causing the team to go deep into its bench. Timberlake didn't even get 15 minutes of fame. He got five minutes of playing time.

"That kid Timberlake had pushed me down earlier in the game, maybe one or two minutes before," Laettner told the Fox Sports Network, which produced a television special on the Kentucky-Duke contest. "So I just made a mental note to get him back and try to be physical with him. And you know, the next time I look up, he's standing right underneath me."

Laettner said he regretted the incident.

"It was a dumb thing to do, but sometimes the emotion of the game, you know, gets into your head too far," he said. "And I got a technical and then that was it."

Timberlake's Kentucky teammates didn't necessarily agree with his smiling and clapping afterward. "[Laettner] stepped on the only guy on the team that wouldn't have got up and clocked him," senior guard Richie Farmer told the Fox Sports Network.

# THE GAME OF MY LIFE
### NCAA EAST REGIONAL FINAL:
### NO. 1 DUKE 104, NO. 6 KENTUCKY 103 (OT)
### MARCH 28, 1992
### BY AMINU TIMBERLAKE

You've got to bring up that Duke game—it's on every year. I see it on ESPN somewhere, or a classic channel. Sometimes I watch it.

Just being a part of it, actually playing in that game was so special. Sometimes I think about how I should have made a reverse layup that I missed, or other things I could've done that would have helped.

But I also think of the joy of being a part of that team. That was a team that really liked each other. That team believed that we could really do it. And to see the strides that team made during the course of the year—we worked together as a team. Coach Pitino wanted us to be the hardest working team in America, and we were. I think we gave people the sense that we could achieve anything.

But sometimes I see that clip—the clip of me and Laettner—and I say, 'Why are they showing this?' It had no real significance in the game. It only added to the drama.

At the time, it looked worse than it was. True—maybe I should've done this or that, but if I had, I would've been ejected, and I don't think that would've been for good for the team at that time. It wasn't even a tap on the stomach. Everybody looks back and says they would have done something, but I couldn't do anything—not in that situation.

So I stood up and clapped. He was caught. I realized he was frustrated and that I had gotten to him.

Yeah, I heard him say I pushed him down. I was like, 'What is he talking about?' I did play him aggressive. I had to. I was, what—30 pounds lighter than he was? But I didn't push him down. I couldn't have.

Still, it was a great, unbelievable game to be a part of. I just wish

I could've done more. But it will still be the most memorable game of my life.

### Statline:

| MIN | FG | FGA | FT | FTA | REB | PF | PTS |
|-----|-----|-----|-----|-----|-----|-----|-----|
| 5 | 0 | 0 | 1 | 2 | 0 | 2 | 1 |

# THE RESULT

Facing elimination and an end to their mini-dynasty, Duke put all of its faith in Laettner's hands. When Pitino elected not to defend the inbounds pass, Duke swingman Grant Hill had a clear path to throw to Laettner. More than 75 feet later, Hill's pass landed in Laettner's hands. Laettner, guarded by Feldhaus and Pelphrey, had time to catch, dribble, spin, and shoot with virtually no opposition.

His 17-footer fell through the net, capping a perfect 10 effort. Laettner went 10-for-10 from the field and 10-for-10 from the free-throw line for 31 points.

For Kentucky, it was the conclusion of a 29-7 season and a year that ended 2.1 seconds away from the Final Four. A week later, Duke, with a record of 34-2, won a second consecutive national championship.

For a group of Kentucky seniors—who would later become known as The Unforgettables—it was the end of their careers. After playing through NCAA probation, the team's memorable run had reached a close.

And the game marked the end of the line for another memorable Kentucky figure. Before the 1991-92 season, radio broadcaster Cawood Ledford, who called play-by-play for the Wildcats for nearly four decades, announced that his 39th year would be his last.

"Heartbreak for Kentucky—a team that fought its heart out," Ledford said over the air that night. "But what a year and what a run for this unbelievable Kentucky basketball team."

Aminu Timberlake's career, on the other hand, had just begun.

# AFTER BLUE

The next season, Kentucky returned to the Final Four. Led by juniors Jamal Mashburn and Travis Ford, and senior Dale Brown,

Kentucky played at a national championship level in 1993 before losing to Michigan's Fab Five in overtime.

"I've still got the Final Four ring," Timberlake says. "Sometimes I still get it out and show it to everyone."

But after seeing his minutes reduced to less than five per game, Timberlake transferred to Southern Illinois the following season, where his statistics improved—so much so that he earned several opportunities to play overseas. And he also met his wife, Lisa.

For five years, Timberlake bounced from Australia to New Zealand, Hong Kong to Korea. He finally quit basketball and moved back to Chicago, where he began his business career. He is now a senior sales manager for Careerbuilder.com.

And sometimes—but not often—people hear his name and remember his Kentucky days. "Sometimes they do—on occasion," he says. "More often than not they only know me for playing for Kentucky. They don't remember the Laettner thing."

And that's the way Timberlake likes it. He enjoys living in Chicago, playing with his three children, and working with his church.

"It was a great run," he says. "At Kentucky, you always wanted to be a No. 1 or No. 2 seed in the tournament. You expected that to happen. You believed it, because if you didn't, it wouldn't happen.

"In my world, the [Laettner stomp] doesn't affect me," he continues. "It comes up sometimes, but from everything I've seen—being a part of the Kentucky tradition, being a part of a Final Four—that's what stood out. That rich tradition is really special."

# CHAPTER 19

# TODD SVOBODA

Some players come to Kentucky as legends: Richie Farmer, Rex Chapman, Winston Bennett. But some players enter the tradition as unknowns, without scouting reports or fanfare. In the UK basketball world, where many fans know incoming players' names before the athletes set foot on campus, a few players fly under the Big Blue Radar. Todd Svoboda is a good example.

During a season in which Rick Pitino recruited the nation's No.1 class, including prep stars Rodrick Rhodes, Tony Delk, Jared Prickett, and Walter McCarty, few had heard much about Kentucky's Todd Svoboda. Even fewer fans could pronounce his name.

But Svoboda (pronounced zva-BO-da) had known fame by the time he arrived at Kentucky. And, in contrast to his teammates, the 6-foot-9 forward's main reason for coming to Lexington centered on academics.

"I was in a college program at [Northern Kentucky University] that called for me to complete three years there, then transfer for my last two years to UK," Svoboda says.

It just so happened that Svoboda—an outstanding student and basketball player from Cincinnati's Princeton High—enrolled at nearby NKU on a basketball scholarship. But he knew that because of academics, he would only play three seasons.

Still, he was following the path his father, Wayne, had set for him. Wayne Svoboda attended Purdue University and majored in chemical engineering while playing tennis. Todd would study chemical engineering at NKU, during which time he became a basketball star at the Division II school. He scored more than 1,000 points in his career, finished fourth on the career rebounds list with 770, and helped establish a program that would later compete for national championships and finish as runners-up in 1996 and 1997.

"For me and my family, we always looked at college as getting an education," Svoboda says. "That's what it's about. Playing sports was a fun thing, a privilege. But you go to college to learn, to earn a degree. Yes, it was difficult leaving NKU and basketball, but I knew I was going to do it."

\* \* \*

Growing up in Cincinnati, there were two college basketball teams Svoboda loved to watch: Nevada Las Vegas and Kentucky. "I loved that fun style they played," he says. "Both those teams really played basketball that was fun to watch."

So when it came time to leave his basketball career at NKU behind, Svoboda thought there may be a chance for him to walk on at Kentucky. "I mentioned it to the coaches at NKU," he says. "They then contacted the coaches at Kentucky."

A lengthy evaluation process followed. Tapes were sent to the UK coaches. Svoboda traveled to Lexington to register for classes and speak with the coaching staff. "At the meeting, the coaches told me they had reviewed the tapes," he says. "They told me, 'Sure, you can walk on. But you may not make the team.'"

Svoboda took the chance. He tried out for a team that featured All-American Jamal Mashburn, All-SEC point guard Travis Ford, and the nation's No.1 recruiting class. Most analysts projected that the team would be ranked in the top five. And most fans predicted the team would return to the Final Four.

Did Svoboda really think he could fit in with this group?

"I didn't know," he says. "But I knew I had to try."

# THE SETTING

"One guy stopped me on campus and said, 'Are you the one who's going to be trying out for the team?' That amazed me," Svoboda says. "A few people did know me as 'The Transfer.' That was something."

Todd Svoboda took a chance that he could make the Kentucky team—and it paid off.

In the summer, Svoboda began working out with other members of the team. "I knew I wasn't the most talented, but I knew I could do some small stuff," he says. "I could run in the open gym. I could be a big body to help in practice. I could be valuable."

Still, the summer conditioning was unlike anything he had ever experienced. Coach Pitino made it clear to Svoboda that the regimen would be the most difficult part of the test. "Coach said, 'We run workouts like NBA workouts,'" Svoboda recalls. "I was like, 'Oh, wow.'"

Svoboda realized early that the workouts created the ultimate team atmosphere. As they endured grueling runs, the individual players began to come together. Svoboda was challenged just like the others.

"I got down to running a mile in four minutes, 57 seconds," he says proudly. "And yes, there were times when people would run until they threw up. Thankfully, though, that didn't happen to me. I was lucky."

But as the months wore on, Svoboda realized the magnitude of the time and energy needed to balance a basketball career at Kentucky with a major in chemical engineering. He considered quitting.

"I'm the type of person that if I'm doing something, I have to do it all the way," he says. "I didn't know if I could."

It was time to call his father. "Dad had been through this," Todd Svoboda says. "He knew what it was like to practice and play and have this major and make it work. And when I called him, he told me that if I quit, I would regret it. He said, 'You won't know if you don't try it.' He told me that I wouldn't want to look back and wish I did this or that. So I kept going."

Svoboda continued working with the team until October, just before practices began. Midnight Madness—the official start of the season—was just around the corner.

One day, Pitino called Svoboda into the coach's office. "I can't guarantee you playing time or a starting position," Pitino told him. "But you've worked hard, and you deserve to make this team."

Svoboda smiled. "I'll take it."

When the formal announcement was made, his new teammates—a group of college and high school All-Americans—mobbed him. They felt he was already a member of the team. This just made it official.

\* \* \*

Svoboda could hardly have picked a better season. After starting out 11-0, Kentucky stormed through the remainder of the regular season, posting a record of 26-3 and winning the SEC tournament championship. *Sports Illustrated* picked Kentucky as the No.1 team in the country before the NCAA Tournament.

Svoboda had become a fan favorite, gaining a few minutes of playing time at the ends of blowout victories. But in a 101-40 win over Tennessee in the first round of the SEC Tournament, Svoboda scored four points and grabbed six rebounds. Tennessee guard Allan Houston, the future NBA star with the New York Knicks, was held to three points in that game. That's right—Svoboda outscored Houston.

But it was in the 1993 NCAA Tournament that Svoboda saw increased playing time. That year, Kentucky set a record for scoring margin on the road to a Final Four appearance. The team outscored its four opponents by an average of 31 points, and Svoboda saw action in each game.

"I remember one fan stopped me in a hotel during that NCAA Tournament run," he says. "The fan asked me why I hadn't taken a three in a game. I just laughed and told him I didn't know. I never thought I would, honestly. Most of the time, with Coach Pitino, you were just thinking about who you were defending."

To get to the Final Four, Kentucky, then No. 2, would have to face No. 11 Florida State—led by Charlie Ward, Sam Cassell, and Bob Sura—in the regional finals. Many predicted a close game. Florida State was quick and played solid defense.

Few, if any, thought Svoboda would get his only three—the mark of Rick Pitino's Kentucky teams—in such an important game.

# THE GAME OF MY LIFE
## NCAA SOUTHEAST REGIONAL FINALS:
## NO. 2 KENTUCKY 106, NO. 11 FLORIDA STATE 81
### MARCH 27, 1993
### BY TODD SVOBODA

It's interesting for me to try to explain the game of my life at Kentucky, because for the majority of the games, I was on the bench. But that team and that game was very special to me.

The game really was a good example of what this team could do. It was close for a while, and some people said it was because we were a little late coming to the arena. We got stuck in some traffic for a little bit, and we only got there about 30 minutes or so before the game started. But Florida State was a great team that year. They did well against defensive pressure because they were such good ball handlers. I remember we didn't lead by very much at halftime, maybe under 10 points.

But in the second half, it seemed like we made a big run, something we were known for throughout that year. The team was so good that people could score a lot of points in a short amount of time. I think we used our size to really take advantage in rebounding, and several players did well setting screens to open up three-point shots.

In the second half, we really opened up a wide margin on them. Threes were falling and the team was really playing like we had all year. It was exciting to know we were that close to going to the Final Four.

I knew that as the score kept widening, I might have a chance to get in. I remember a lot of people had great games. Mashburn. Prickett. The team was amazing on that entire run to the Final Four. But around the eight-minute mark, the fans started chanting. That season, sometimes they would chant "We want Todd," and they started up with about eight minutes to go.

But Coach Pitino would never immediately do what the crowd wanted. He would wait and eventually he would come over and tell me to go in for someone. As the crowd was screaming, he came over and told me, and I stood up. The place seemed to go crazy—I could hardly hear because the place was so nuts.

So I went into the game—I don't even know who I went in for—and the only thing I'm thinking is who I have to guard, because I want to do something productive. I knew this was probably my last chance to get into a game. This was special, too, because my dad and sister were able to be there in Charlotte. My mom is deceased, but my family is really close and it was nice for them to be there. I wanted to get in the game and do well.

As the game wore on, I was able to contribute, but I remember I missed a shot. I knew that some of my teammates were trying to get me shots. As time wore down, it became obvious we were going to the Final Four and we were all just having fun.

But the seconds were ticking away, and time had almost expired when Jeff Brassow got the ball. Brassow and I were roommates, and the time was almost gone, so I knew he was going to the basket and he was going to kick it to me.

I knew I was going to be shooting, and that I was behind the three-point line, right in front of our bench. I was on the right wing, and [Brassow] got me the ball.

I let it go. And when I hit that shot, time ran out and the whole bench had their arms up in the air, and they jumped off the ground.

There was not one person sitting down. Everyone was up and cheering. They were cheering for me, for hitting that shot. That's what makes it all worthwhile.

That right there is why I picked this game.

## Statline:

| MIN | FG | FGA | 3FG | 3FGA | PTS |
|-----|----|----|-----|------|-----|
| 1 | 1 | 2 | 1 | 1 | 3 |

# THE RESULT

After The Unforgettables' 1992 season ended on Christian Laettner's miracle shot, Kentucky basketball was back. Kentucky was on its way to the Final Four.

In 1993, Cats fans were smiling after a big shot in a regional final—a shot by Svoboda. "I remember that after I hit that shot, Coach Pitino walked off the court, and he had a smile worth 1,000 words," Svoboda says. "That three capped off the run we had in the tourney. That was a great feeling."

The team cut down the nets and celebrated. But a week later, the team's phenomenal run would come to an end. The Kentucky team lost in the Final Four to Michigan's Fab Five, featuring Chris Webber and Jalen Rose. Kentucky star Jamal Mashburn had fouled out, and the Wildcats could not keep up in overtime. The team finished with a record of 30-4.

And while the national championship would elude them, the Wildcats did earn a Final Four ring. "I still have it," Svoboda says. In his one season of eligibility, Svoboda was able to join college basketball's most storied program on a Final Four run.

"We were the best conditioned team in the country," Svoboda says. "Pitino was one of the best coaches, teachers, and basketball minds I've ever been around. You should have seen him after a loss. He was always sore—and we would work hard after a loss. But he could get the most out of us."

# AFTER BLUE

Svoboda now uses his Kentucky degree everyday with Lexmark International in Lexington. He also married a UK gymnast. The couple has two children.

After graduating a year after the Final Four run, Svoboda went to work in Florida before returning to the Bluegrass State. "I missed it here," he says.

Another thing he misses is the competition of his playing days. "I'm in research and development," he says. "We're trying to develop the next great laser printer. I go in, I work hard, but I do miss the competition."

He lives in the countryside, and neighbors aren't that close by. But he does get recognized, he says, from time to time. People will remember him for his one year at UK—and his three-pointer.

In his office, Svoboda has a picture that ran in the newspaper the day after the Florida State game. The image shows Svoboda shooting his three-pointer. In the background, every player on the bench is cheering him on. "Oh yes, I have it," he says. "And I still have my piece of net somewhere in the attic.

"It's something I can always tell my kids and my grandkids," he says. "My family was proud. I was just thankful I made the decision that I made."

# CHAPTER 20

# TRAVIS FORD

Many people sold Travis Ford short—emphasis on the short. At 5-foot-9, Ford looked like he may have been a bit undersized to play basketball. Or maybe he looked a bit too heavy at times. Or maybe he just looked like he should be swinging a golf club rather than crossing over defenders.

Well, he played golf and baseball, too, but basketball was his love. And he wanted to play for the University of Kentucky more than anything. As a senior at North Hopkins High School in Madisonville, Ford averaged 31.7 points and eight assists per game. He earned *Parade* All-America honors and was MVP of the McDonald's Capitol Classic.

Despite all of his great qualities, Ford's timing was a bit off. When he graduated from high school, Kentucky was crowded with guards, including head coach Eddie Sutton's son, Sean, and Kentucky high school legend Richie Farmer. But other schools came calling.

"I was always a big basketball fan and a big Kentucky fan," Ford says. "I always wanted to play or to work on my game."

When he was young, his father, Eddie, who coached the local junior AAU All-Stars, instructed him in the fundamentals of the game. "It was all about ball handling, dribbling, and shooting the right way," Ford says. "You had to have all of your fundamentals right."

Every day, even as a kid, Ford practiced a stringent regimen of drills. "There was a workout every day," he says. "I had an agenda, and I knew how long I would work on each part of my game. If you were organized, and if you had a system to get better, you would get better."

Ford studied UK star Kyle Macy's free-throw form. He noted Rex Chapman's explosive first step to the basket. "I followed both of those guys—they were my heroes," Ford says. "That's who I wanted to be."

But like Macy, who transferred to Kentucky from Purdue, it took Ford a little longer to fulfill his dream. He decided to attend the University of Missouri; it seemed like a good fit. The system highlighted his skills, and playing time was readily available. After putting up good numbers as a freshman, Ford was named to the Big Eight's all-freshman team. His future looked bright. But after Ford's freshman season, the NCAA placed Missouri on probation. It was time to leave.

While playing at Missouri, Ford followed Kentucky's progress under their new coach, Rick Pitino. Ford made it clear that he wanted to transfer.

In his book *Full-Court Pressure,* Pitino said Ford's father called the UK to express Travis' interest in Wildcats basketball. "I told him we were interested," Pitino wrote. "Then [Eddie Ford] said Travis was going to visit North Carolina. Then LSU was going to send a private plane to pick [Travis] up."

According to Pitino, the rest of the conversation went like this: "Well, let me say this, Eddie. If [Travis] takes one step on Carolina's campus, he will not be given a scholarship to the University of Kentucky."

Pitino told Eddie Ford that UK had passed on recruiting high school All-Americans Travis Best and Cory Alexander because they wanted Travis Ford. "I don't believe transfers should ever leave a program unless they have a program to go to," Pitino wrote. "So, if you're not sure what you're looking for," he told Eddie, "Kentucky's not the place for [Travis]."

The next day, Travis Ford announced his commitment to Kentucky.

# THE SETTING

Ford sat out during the 1990-91 season, Kentucky's final year under NCAA probation. Four beloved seniors—John Pelphrey, Sean Woods, Deron Feldhaus, and Richie Farmer—and one All-America

Travis Ford (No. 5) left Kentucky, then came back, before helping to lead the Wildcats to the Final Four.

candidate, Jamal Mashburn, would be returning for the 1991-92 season. The year looked to be one to remember.

Travis Ford would play a small part, backing up Woods, the starting point guard. Some of the players called Ford "Doogie," as in "Doogie Howser," in reference to the television show and Ford's lack of height. Apparently, the moniker didn't stick. Maybe Ford schooled too many teammates.

In 1992, the Wildcats went 29-7, won the SEC East and the SEC Tournament, and lost to Duke in the greatest NCAA Tournament game ever played. They just missed a trip to the Final Four.

In 1993, Ford became the team's starting point guard. He played alongside All-American Jamal Mashburn, standout freshmen Rodrick Rhodes and Jared Prickett, shooting guard Dale Brown, and center Rodney Dent. The team would quickly become known as one of the best in the country.

The Wildcats began the season 11-0 and earned the No.1 national ranking. Along the way, Ford had monster games. He and Jamal Mashburn scored 29 points each in a thrilling 81-78 win over fourth-ranked Indiana. The Wildcats torched ninth-ranked Louisville by 20 points and 11th-ranked Vanderbilt by 15 points.

Ford set the Kentucky record for three-pointers made in a season, canning 101 of 191 for a ridiculous 52.9 percent. The team rolled all the way to the Final Four, destroying its opponents—including 19th-ranked Utah, 16th-ranked Wake Forest, and 11th-ranked Florida State—by an average of 31 points, the greatest average margin for a Final Four team in NCAA history. Ford was named the region's Most Valuable Player.

But the run would end in New Orleans, the site of the year's Final Four. This time, it was Michigan and their Fab Five starters, including Chris Webber, Juwan Howard, and Jalen Rose, who defeated Kentucky, 81-78, in overtime. "That's still a tough game to think about," Ford says.

* * *

After Jamal Mashburn left college basketball for the NBA, many assumed Kentucky's next season would be a rebuilding one. But the 1993-94 installment still had Travis Ford, an All-SEC point guard, as well as Rhodes, shooting guard Tony Delk, Prickett, powerful center Rodney Dent, reserves Jeff Brassow, Gimel Martinez, Andre Riddick, and Chris Harrison, and newcomers Walter McCarty (who took the court after sitting out his freshman season), Jeff Sheppard, and Anthony Epps.

The team was experienced, athletic, and deep. It appeared the Wildcats had the potential to be the best in the nation.

After an early season-opening victory over seventh-ranked Louisville, 78-70, Kentucky held the No. 1 ranking for two games. Then the Wildcats fell to rival Indiana, 96-84. It would take nine games before the Wildcats saw defeat again. And included in that streak was a game in Lahaina, Hawaii, during which three pint-sized ballers played bigger than their bodies.

# THE GAME OF MY LIFE
## MAUI INVITATIONAL CLASSIC CHAMPIONSHIP:
### NO. 3 KENTUCKY 93, NO. 13 ARIZONA 92
### DECEMBER 23, 1993
#### BY TRAVIS FORD

I've always said this game is the most exciting game I've ever played in. It really was, for a lot of reasons. It was the beginning of the season, and both teams really felt like they were good enough to make a run at the national championship. Plus, they had those two premiere guards—Khalid Reeves and Damon Stoudamire. But we were two really different teams.

We had not played exceptionally well going into that tournament in Maui. We were still trying to figure out our roles and become consistent. But Arizona had played very well coming into that game. They were a senior-led team who knew what they were going to do. They were going to run you up and down the floor, and they were going to outscore you and out-quick you. And that's the way it went, back and forth, it seemed for the whole game.

There wasn't much defense, because no one on either side could guard one another. I would hit a three, and then Damon or Khalid would come down and hit a three.

Really, all of us guards were the smallest guys on the court. And really, no one could stop us. Still, we felt good, because we always had the lead. It seemed like we led the entire game. At the half, we were up pretty good [49-41], and we just wanted to go out and keep going.

All of us were hitting shots. Tony Delk hit so many big shots for us. But we couldn't stop Arizona. It got to the point where we had to keep making all of our shots to keep up with them. And in that little gym, with under 3,000 fans there, it was so hot. Most of the crowd was split—Kentucky and Arizona—and they were so loud. That's why it was so exciting.

There was a big three I hit with about 1:30 to go. It was a play Coach Pitino drew up in the dirt where I came off a screen and was there and I hit it. We thought things were really working when that play worked.

We had a lead, and Arizona had what we thought would be the last shot. But we fouled Khalid, and he went to the line. Of course he hit both of them. So they had the lead, and we had the last chance.

Originally, I think the play was supposed to go to Tony Delk. But Rhodes got the ball and brought it up real quick. It was so emotionally draining because the game was so close, and you wanted to get your season off on a good note.

So when Rhodes shot it, almost from half court, all I thought was, 'If we make it, we win.' I didn't even think we would have time for a tip, but that's what you always hope for.

So then the ball comes off to the left and Jeff is right there, of course, and he just reaches up and puts it back through. To fight that hard and have that happen to Jeff, it really was the best way for it to end for us.

It was a surprise; it was exhilarating. And then everybody ran out to the court. I don't think any of us could believe we'd won.

### Statline:

| MIN | FG | FGA | 3FG | 3FGA | A | REB | PTS |
|-----|-----|-----|-----|------|---|-----|-----|
| 36 | 8 | 17 | 7 | 14 | 5 | 4 | 25 |

# THE RESULT

Bill Raftery, the color commentator working the game for ESPN, could be heard shouting through the melee: "Bras-SOW! Bras-SOW! Bras-SOW!"

Jeff Brassow's tip at the buzzer won the Maui Invitational for Kentucky and sent the Wildcats running onto the court. Pitino threw his arms around Brassow. Then Ford found the group, and together they jumped near midcourt. ESPN had an Instant Classic game that would be watched again and again over the next few decades.

Ford became the only player to win two Maui Invitational Classics.

Because a team can only be invited to the tournament once every four seasons, it was an improbable achievement. But Ford's team also won the title when he was a freshman at Missouri.

Years later, Brassow is still asked about his title-winning tip. "Honestly, 95 percent luck and five percent being in the right spot," Brassow told the *Lexington Herald-Leader.* "It just bounced off my hand and into the basket."

But fans sometimes forget who kept the Wildcats in the game. Travis Ford finished with 25 points after sinking seven three-pointers. He also chipped in four rebounds and five assists. Ford earned the MVP award for his efforts. Brassow had six points, Martinez scored eight points, Delk played well with 18 points, Rhodes scored 12 points, and Prickett finished with 16 points. The victory was a team effort.

* * *

Unfortunately for UK, the season peaked in Maui. Dent injured his knee, depleting the team at center, and Rhodes' lack of consistency became a problem between himself and Pitino. The team lacked height, muscle, and a go-to guy.

Ford tried his best, averaging 11.3 points and bringing leadership to the team. He won another conference tournament Most Valuable Player award when Kentucky returned as the SEC Tournament champion.

But in the NCAA Tournament, seventh-ranked Kentucky appeared young and unable to overcome its weaknesses. The Wildcats lost to No. 21 Marquette, 75-63, in the second round.

# AFTER BLUE

After graduating from Kentucky, Ford earned a spot in training camp with the NBA's Golden State Warriors. But he was cut, and he quickly realized he would much rather be a coach. "It's always been something I've wanted to do," he says.

Before he began his coaching career, Hollywood came calling. Disney was making a movie about a basketball player who dies prematurely but returns to help his former team win a collegiate championship. The movie called for a small point guard who could shoot.

Travis Ford got the part. And fans can still watch his performance in *The Sixth Man*.

Ford landed his first coaching job at Campbellsville, the NAIA school in Kentucky. After three years, Ford's team posted a 23-11 record and earned a spot in the NAIA National Tournament. That led to Ford's next job at Eastern Kentucky, where, in five years, he won the Ohio Valley Conference Tournament title and took the Colonels to their first NCAA Tournament in more than 25 years. Fittingly, the Colonels were matched up against Kentucky. EKU fought hard before falling, 72-64.

Now, Ford coaches at the University of Massachusetts, where he is rebuilding the Minutemen. He lives with his wife, Heather, a former Kentucky swimmer, and their three children.

Ford sites former coaches Rick Pitino, Billy Donovan, Herb Sendek, and Tubby Smith as his major influences. But Ford's teams play in a style reminiscent of his days at UK under Pitino—fast.

"All of my coaches have been major influences to me," he says. "I just hope I can have some of the same successes they've had." And judging from his success as a player, it's unlikely that Travis Ford will disappoint.

# CHAPTER 21

# WALTER McCARTY

Ever since his boyhood days in Evansville, Indiana, Walter McCarty could fill the room with his strong, smooth voice. But no one imagined that his athletic prowess would eventually equal his vocal talent.

He did not play on the Harrison High varsity basketball squad as a freshman. As a sophomore, he averaged six points. But things rapidly changed at that point: McCarty grew to nearly 7 feet tall. All the while, he maintained his quickness, shooting ability, and soft hands.

By the time he was a senior, McCarty had developed into what many recruiting experts called the most versatile big man in the Midwest. He was named a *Parade* All-American and drew interest from big-time college basketball programs, including Kentucky.

"He was a late bloomer," Rick Pitino said in his book *Full-Court Pressure*. "I felt he was one of the three or four best prospects in the country."

Unfortunately, McCarty followed some bad advice from a high school guidance counselor and lacked the core classes necessary to attend college. Any college program that took the talented player would have to wait a year for him to play. Many schools backed off.

"What are you going to do?" Pitino said. "He comes from a good family, and we didn't feel it was a gamble."

Joy Lindsey, McCarty's mother, worked at a factory in Kentucky across the river from Evansville. She encouraged her son to attend UK. McCarty ultimately chose the Wildcats over Purdue and his hometown Evansville Purple Aces. And even though he couldn't play during his freshman season, he would put his voice to good use, singing the national anthem before games.

"I always loved Kentucky," McCarty says. "I always loved that style of play, and I remember thinking I could see myself perform in that kind of style."

Kentucky boasted the No. 1 recruiting class for the 1992-93 season. The phenomenal newcomers included Walter McCarty, Tony Delk, Rodrick Rhodes, and Jared Prickett,

# THE SETTING

McCarty was academically ineligible to participate in Kentucky's run to the 1993 Final Four. He watched and waited for his opportunity to shine.

Coming into the 1993-94 campaign, many expected the Wildcats to compete for another conference championship and make another successful appearance in the NCAA Tournament. Rhodes, Delk, and Prickett were entering their sophomore seasons, along with talented center Rodney Dent and point guard Travis Ford. The team featured a stellar bench, including Gimel Martinez, Jeff Brassow, Andre Riddick, Chris Harrison, Anthony Epps, and Jeff Sheppard.

But no player could fill Jamal Mashburn's shoes, and Rhodes did not step up as the go-to player the team needed. After just 11 games, Dent suffered a season-ending injury, leaving a huge hole in the middle of the team. Perimeter shooting, which was already a staple of Rick Pitino's teams, would become even more important.

The Wildcats started off 11-1 and ascended to the No. 1 ranking in the country early in the season. But the Dent injury was costly. As Martinez and Riddick did yeoman's work filling in for the starting center, the team posted an 8-2 record in SEC play.

Then the Wildcats hit the wall. In a murderous stretch of the schedule, the No. 7 Wildcats faced 11th-ranked Massachusetts in New Jersey (a 67-64 win), traveled back to Lexington for a date with the third-ranked Arkansas Razorbacks (a 90-82 loss), and flew to Syracuse, New York, to play the 14th-ranked Orangemen (a 93-85 loss). It was the first time in two years a Pitino-led UK squad had dropped two consecutive games. And the immediate future didn't

---

Walter McCarty had a reputation for hitting clutch shots and was a vital part of the team's run to the 1996 NCAA title.

look much better.

The 11th-ranked Wildcats were slated to travel to Baton Rouge to face the unranked LSU Tigers in a late-night ESPN televised game. The game began at 9:30 eastern time. Fans were concerned. Kentucky had not won in Baton Rouge since 1988.

"I was just working my way into getting consistent minutes," McCarty remembers. "Those losses—the one to Syracuse and the other to Arkansas—those were the types of games that prepare you for the [NCAA] Tournament. But they were tough losses. We were in a rut, and we knew it had been a while since a Kentucky team had lost three in a row."

Yet many Kentucky fans went to sleep that night thinking the Wildcats had done just that—lost their third consecutive game. But the morning after what would become known as the Mardi Gras Miracle, those fans would never go to sleep on Kentucky again. And neither would LSU.

# THE GAME OF MY LIFE
## NO. 11 KENTUCKY 99, LSU 95
### FEBRUARY 15, 1994
### BY WALTER MCCARTY

We did not want to lose another game. Part of it was because we didn't want to have to face a practice from Coach when we had a three-game losing streak.

We knew going in who their great players were—[Clarence] Ceasar and [Ronnie] Henderson—and in the first half they were just lights out. I know one of them had like seven threes, and I think we were down 26 at the half. We were playing a zone defense and they just kept shooting and making shots. At halftime, we didn't know what to say to each other. We'd never seen anything like that. We just wanted to go back out and try and make it better.

Guys were cramping up because it was so hot down there. And our confidence started cramping up, too. Everything felt like it was sinking. The LSU players were so upbeat, so excited. I remember one player said something to one of the ESPN cameras at halftime—he said hello to his mom or something like that—and that really made us mad because it was like the game was over. That lit a fire in us.

I'm not going to lie and say we knew we could win. Really, what we wanted to do was come back and fight. We wanted to work hard and make it respectable. That was our goal because we knew that Coach Pitino was going to be so angry at us. We were scared of him. We knew he'd make practice terrible for us if we didn't keep working.

But we did know one thing. We knew that if we had any time left, we could make a run. That was our system. We'd done it before, and we knew we had a run in us. We had to make threes and create turnovers.

In the second half, they just continued making shots. And we just kept playing and thinking it had to turn around for us sometime. It eventually reached a 31-point lead.

Then we started catching some breaks. Delk and Martinez were fighting through slumps and hit some shots. Then Travis hit one. And Gimel, Delk, Jeff Brassow, and I—really everyone—started stepping up.

LSU was wearing down, and you knew they thought they had already won the game. But we started hitting shots, and we were getting turnovers. We would foul them, and they were missing free throws. It all started to come together for us. Then you looked up and we were down 15 or 12, and we knew we were back.

I felt like I was doing a lot of good out there. I was playing good defense, which allowed me to be out on the floor. But I was also rebounding and getting easy buckets and making threes.

There were some shots we made—three-pointers—that were from very far out, but they went in. Jeff Brassow made some huge shots. And then the score was under 10 points. Then it was down to a two-point lead.

Then it seemed like each team turned the ball over a couple of times before we got it back with under 20 seconds to go. Coach Pitino then drew up a play for Tony Delk. That play was for a three for us to take the lead, but in the end, just before we went back out on to the court, Coach said that if Tony needed help, he had me in the corner.

That's how it happened. Tony found me with the ball right in front of our bench, and the shot went in.

That execution comes from being prepared, being ready, and practicing. Our confidence came from our practices. Any one of us would have hit that shot.

That shot deflated them. Once we took the lead, we knew we had them. We knew we had their number. Afterward, they were just stunned. They couldn't speak. You'll never see another game like that.

### Statline:

| FG | FGA | 3FG | 3FGA | FT | FTA | REB | PF | BL | ST | PTS |
|----|-----|-----|------|----|-----|-----|----|----|----|-----|
| 9 | 14 | 4 | 7 | 1 | 2 | 8 | 3 | 2 | 2 | 23 |

# THE RESULT

Travis Ford hit two free throws in the end to seal the 99-95 comeback win. The Wildcats mobbed one another at center court, celebrating a win each player would remember for years to come.

Kentucky outscored LSU 62-27 in the second half, including a 9-0 run to end the game. Over the last 12 minutes, Kentucky hit 12 of 23 three-pointers, while LSU missed 11 of 12 free throws. Henderson scored 36 points (with eight three-pointers) and Ceasar chipped in 32 points, but neither came away as winners.

LSU coach Dale Brown praised the Wildcats for their effort. According to the *NCAA Basketball Yearbook,* the 31-point comeback was the second largest in the history of the NCAA.

Like many other Kentucky fans, Steven Lindsey, Walter McCarty's father, fell asleep during the LSU game. He thought a UK blowout was not worth seeing. "I called home after the game," McCarty says, "and I had to tell him what had happened."

\* \* \*

The 1993-94 Wildcats finished 27-7 and won the SEC Tournament championship. But a promising NCAA Tournament run was halted in a second-round upset loss to Marquette.

One year later, when Kentucky trailed 91-82 with 1:39 remaining in overtime of the SEC Tournament championship game against Arkansas, Delk and McCarty called on the memory of the Mardi Gras Miracle. They knew anything could happen.

Again, Kentucky bounced back for a thrilling win, claiming another SEC Tourney crown. "We had come back from 31 down before," McCarty says. "We knew we could come back at any time. It was always in the backs of our minds. We knew we could overcome any kind of adversity."

The next year, the Wildcats would cut down the nets after finishing the season with a record of 34-2 and winning the 1996 national championship. "We talked a lot about sacrifice on that team," McCarty says of the national champions. "We trusted each other. And we all really loved each other. We were like family, and we were able to do amazing things."

# AFTER BLUE

After capping off his hugely successful Kentucky career with a national title, McCarty was selected 19th in the first round of the NBA Draft by the New York Knicks. He also found a home with the Boston Celtics for a few seasons under his former coach, Rick Pitino.

McCarty was a fan favorite in Boston. Celtics announcers fueled his popularity by shouting "I love Walter!" when McCarty played well. He now resides in Boston with his wife and two daughters.

But basketball isn't his only interest. In 1998, McCarty auditioned for the leading role in Spike Lee's basketball movie *He Got Game,* starring Denzel Washington. Although the lead went to then-Milwaukee Bucks star Ray Allen, McCarty received a plum speaking part as Allen's character's friend.

And in 2003, McCarty fulfilled a lifelong dream: he released an album of R&B and soul tracks entitled *Moment for Love.*

In 2006, after playing for the New York Knicks, the Boston Celtics, the Phoenix Suns, and the Los Angeles Clippers, McCarty found himself without a team. In 2007, McCarty joined Pitino's Louisville staff as an assistant coach.

"Basketball has done so much for me," McCarty says. "I am able to have all of these opportunities because of the sport." And no game stands out in his memory more than the Mardi Gras Miracle. "People still tell me they've seen the game on television somewhere," he says. "I have the game at home, too.

"It's something that stays with you, even in the NBA," he says. "Whenever you think something can't be done, it gets brought up. After that, you know you can do just about anything."

# CHAPTER 22

# TONY DELK

As a kid, Tony Delk played basketball with his brothers—some of whom were 20 years older than Tony. They used an old hoop and played on the hard dirt in the backyard of their Tennessee home.

Delk had to make up for his lack of height somehow, so he developed a high-arching shot, one that would clear taller defenders and—more often than not—find its way through the bottom of the net. Sometimes he shot over trees. And sometimes his brothers seemed as big as those trees.

"That's where I learned to play basketball," he says. "I credit my family with teaching me the game, helping me develop my talent. They made me better, stronger, faster. Sometimes they'd make me run a mile before we played. I was so tired, but it made me better."

And he would always watch his beloved Memphis State Tigers play. "Penny Hardaway—one of my favorite players," Delk says. "I loved the way they played. Sometimes I would stay up and watch UNLV play, too, because they ran up and down the court. I loved to watch those teams."

Delk would eventually become a basketball star in his hometown of Brownsville, located just 40 minutes northeast of Memphis. "My coach and my teammates really let me take over," he says. "I really credit them with letting me show people what I could do."

Delk scored more than 70 points in one high school game. He became a McDonald's All-American, and that's how he first met a future Syracuse star—a big man named John Wallace.

Memphis State was impressed, as was Arkansas and the University of Kentucky. But the Wildcats had one thing the other teams did not: Billy Donovan.

Donovan, Kentucky's assistant coach and head recruiter, had quickly established himself as a leader in the recruiting world. A former player and deadly shooter at Providence College under coach Rick Pitino, "Billy the Kid" Donovan led his team to the Final Four in 1987. He could relate to young college players.

"He sent me letters every day," Delk says. "All of the recruiters came after me hard. Mike Anderson at Arkansas was very good. But Billy and me, we just bonded. He made me want to be at Kentucky."

As part of the number-one-ranked recruiting class in the country, Delk had trouble fitting in as a freshman. With fellow newcomer Rodrick Rhodes establishing himself as a viable scoring threat, Delk, who averaged 4.6 points per game while struggling to move to the point guard position, received minimal playing time. But the former Brownsville star had potential, scoring 18 points against South Carolina and 15 points against Tennessee. His freshman season ended with a loss to Michigan's Fab Five in the Final Four.

"That was a tough year," Delk says. "But through it all, Coach Donovan was there for me. Sometimes we would just spend time shooting in the gym together. He had a way of making you feel better."

Delk's career began to improve during his sophomore year, when he was moved to his natural shooting guard position. He became the team's leading scorer and go-to player, averaging 16.6 points per game. As a junior, Delk scored 16.7 points per game, dropping 31 points on Arkansas in a 94-92 loss. But that season ended on the sourest of notes—a 13-point loss to fourth-ranked North Carolina in the regional finals. Kentucky missed its chance to return to the Final Four.

# THE SETTING

According to UK players, Coach Pitino attributed the 1995 North Carolina loss to the Wildcats' selfishness. It was a game that many players felt they should've won—if they'd played smarter. North Carolina baited the Wildcats into shooting too many three-pointers, most of which were bad shots.

---

Tony Delk was the sweet-shooting guard Kentucky needed to deliver a sixth national title.

"He lashed out at us," Delk remembers of Pitino. "He told us, 'Next year, if you're not dedicated to the game, you need to transfer.' It set the tone for the next season. He knew we had it in us. He just wanted us to realize it."

The team changed. Rhodes transferred to Southern California. High school All-Americans Ron Mercer and Wayne Turner joined the Wildcats. Derek Anderson, a transfer from Ohio State, became eligible.

The Wildcats featured a talent-packed roster, which included Tony Delk, Walter McCarty, Antoine Walker, Mark Pope, Jeff Sheppard, Anthony Epps, and Allen Edwards.

In the summer of 1995, the Wildcats fostered team chemistry during an overseas trip to Italy. "That's where the season really started for us," Delk says. "We bonded there, playing and getting used to a new country."

When the college basketball season began, many onlookers believed Kentucky possessed the talent to win the national championship. The Associated Press voted the Wildcats No. 1 in the country. But would there be enough basketballs to go around in Lexington? How could Rick Pitino manage all of those egos?

"Coach Pitino said it from the beginning," Delk says. "He said we could be a really special team if we set our egos aside."

The toughest part was practice. "Practicing two to three hours against these guys was really hard," he says. "The competition made us all that much better. Coach Pitino recruited guys every year that would come in and challenge you for your job. But mentally and physically, that got us prepared."

The season began with a convincing 12-point win over 14th-ranked Maryland. But on November 28, Kentucky faced seventh-ranked Massachusetts. The two teams would chase one another throughout the regular season.

In the late November faceoff, UMass won by 10 points, largely due to a spectacular performance by All-American Marcus Camby. UMass exposed Kentucky's weak defense on the front line, and the guards handled Kentucky's full-court pressure admirably.

After flirting with the notion of moving Delk to point guard again, Pitino placed him at shooting guard. Epps and Turner handled the point guard roles. Slowly the team began to gel.

* * *

Twenty-seven consecutive victories later, the Kentucky Wildcats had won the SEC regular-season title. Only a loss to Mississippi State in the SEC Tournament final blemished the record. Coincidentally, UMass had also lost just one game and entered the NCAA Tournament with the No.1 ranking.

No. 2 Kentucky rolled to the Final Four. The interior defense had gotten better, and UK was a force to be reckoned with. The much-anticipated UK-UMass rematch was staged in the national semifinal.

Delk and the Wildcats played inspired basketball against John Calipari's Massachusetts team. Camby scored 25 points and eight rebounds, but Kentucky's team executed a superb performance. Delk scored 20 points, and seven Wildcats players scored six-plus points. Pope hit clutch free throws down the stretch to seal the win.

"Losing to UMass in the second game of the year, it was big for us to beat them in that game," Delk says. "But for us, we knew our job wasn't finished. We had one more game to go—and that was the most important game."

# THE GAME OF MY LIFE
## NCAA CHAMPIONSHIP:
## NO. 2 KENTUCKY 76, NO. 15 SYRACUSE 67
## APRIL 1, 1996
### BY TONY DELK

I couldn't sleep at all the night before the national championship game. It was the most nervous I'd ever been before a game.

Our team knew we had done something big when we beat the UMass team. That was a great team. But we also knew we had to come right back, and not have a letdown when we played UMass.

I was nervous. Of course I was. It was a big game, the biggest game. But it was what we'd worked for to get to that point. Another thing I was thinking was that this would be my last college game. And I just kept telling myself, 'Tony, you've got to go out on top.' This was my first and last opportunity to win a championship.

Before the game, Coach Pitino didn't say very much. He knew he didn't have to. He told us that we'd gotten to this point because we'd put our egos aside, and we worked hard. He said, "You know what to do. We have to come back to this locker room as champions." That was all we needed.

I was glad the game was held in New Jersey. This was the Meadowlands—an arena, not a dome. And I'd never shot very well inside a dome before, so I kind of felt good because of the environment. There were just 20,000 fans there, and it felt like a home game, not a big tournament game. But everybody had pictured it to be a blowout. We were nervous because we were supposed to win. Syracuse had nothing to lose.

I remember feeling great in the first half. We knew it was going to be difficult to run away from them because they would slow it down and play that zone defense. But I kept finding open threes—six in the first half for my 18 points. And we had a lead on them. I was in one of those times when I was in a good, comfortable place. I was shooting good, and we were playing our game. And we felt really good that we were just a half away from winning a championship.

But they were a team of really good players. Their point guard, [Lazarus] Sims, handled our pressure really well. We knew we had to keep at him though, try to tire him out. And John Wallace and I had known each other since we were friends in high school. Our plan as a team was to let him score his 20 and grab his 10, but shut everyone else down.

Every shot we took in the second half was a pressure shot. I knew they were going to be keying on me, so it opened it up for my teammates. Ron Mercer stepped up and got his threes, too, and got 20 points. That was it—no team could just prepare for one player. There were so many good players on our team; none of us averaged a lot of minutes because everyone got in. Everyone could play.

But I remember that one moment everyone has seen. I was in the corner, right in front of our bench, and I shot up a three. [Syracuse guard Todd Burgan] ran at me, and I knew it may have been a bad shot, so I tried to get the contact and fall down to get the foul. The three went in. That was number seven.

And I got fouled. I remember my teammates on the bench jumped all on me. McCarty and Derek Anderson gave me five. Then I hit the free throw. That was a big moment for us in that game.

But that Syracuse team never went away. They were so good, they cut the lead to two with just a few minutes left. But [Walter McCarty] rebounded and scored off a big miss and Derek [Anderson] hit a three. We were on our way. I remember I got the last basket of the game—a layup. Then we started celebrating.

### Statline:

| MIN | FG | FGA | 3FG | 3FGA | FT | FTA | REB | PTS |
|-----|-----|-----|-----|------|-----|-----|-----|-----|
| 37 | 8 | 20 | 7 | 12 | 1 | 2 | 7 | 24 |

# THE RESULT

Kentucky won its sixth national championship—and second title since 1958—on the strength of its perimeter shooting. Delk, the tournament's Most Outstanding Player, tied a title-game record with his seven three-pointers, and the team set a title-game record with 12 total threes. Pitino fulfilled his promise to the Kentucky fans in his seventh season: he delivered a championship.

"We put our names in history," Delk says. "I think we were the best team in the history of college basketball."

After the game, the team's bus rolled into Rupp Arena in front of 23,000 screaming fans. "It was an unreal feeling," Delk says. "Just crazy. I had so many different emotions. I thought, 'Man, this started in Italy, back in the summer. All this work we put in finally paid off.'"

But this championship meant more than just the perfect ending of a season. "We got our title, but more importantly, we put Kentucky basketball back on the map," he says. "Sometimes, when you haven't won in a while, you're forgotten. We made people remember who the best program in college basketball was. And when programs win, you can keep getting the best recruits.

"Just to go out on top, to win your last game, that was the best," he says. "I got to go off into the sunset. Not too many people get to say that."

# AFTER BLUE

"We were picked in the preseason as the No. 1 team, and we went out as the No. 1 team," Delk says. "It was an unbelievable run."

Delk parlayed his superstar status in college into a productive professional career. Although he was criticized as being too small to play shooting guard and not talented enough to play the point, he was drafted No. 16 by the Charlotte Hornets in the first round of the 1996 NBA draft, joining teammates Walker, McCarty, and Pope as draft picks. Delk traveled throughout the league, stopping in Golden State, Phoenix, Atlanta, Dallas, Sacramento, and Boston before finally settling in Detroit for the 2005-06 season.

In the NBA, Delk became known as a reliable backup scorer who could play spot duty at the point guard position. He made history with a 53-point game for the Phoenix Suns against Sacramento in

2001.

"Coach P got players ready for the next level," Delk says. "I can't complain. I lasted a lot longer than anyone expected."

In 2006, after 10 years in the NBA, Delk was prepared to finish the second year of a two-year deal with the Detroit Pistons. But a team in Greece offered him a more lucrative contract, and Delk left the NBA behind.

"Everyone always told me I was too small or couldn't play this position," he says. "But they can't measure your heart. And you can't teach heart. I knew I could play, and I didn't care what anybody said. I did it for 10 years, and I made a lot of friends."

Delk is enjoying spending his time overseas as his career winds down. "Who else can say they're spending time in the Mediterranean?" he says. "This is another experience."

But he misses his wife and three daughters, who live in Atlanta. "I know I only have a few more years left," Delk says. "Then I go home and start the next chapter.

"Maybe it's me knowing there's only a few years left, but I've been looking back on my career," he says. "That UK team was special. And I've had a lot of great times."

# CHAPTER 23

# DEREK ANDERSON

Derek Anderson didn't succumb to drugs and alcohol while growing up in Louisville's tough West End. Rather, at 12 years old, Anderson peddled candy to make ends meet. His single mother was constantly trying to find employment, so Anderson was frequently on his own. That is, until he wandered to the playgrounds and began to play basketball. He became fast friends with other young players—many of whom evolved into Kentucky high school basketball legends.

As a high school freshman, Anderson averaged 10 points per game for the Doss Dragons. Anderson's personal life became more stable after he moved in with his uncle, and as a sophomore he averaged 15 points, five rebounds, and five assists per game.

But during his high school basketball days, Anderson was overshadowed by some of his former playground buddies. Ballard's DeJuan Wheat, Louisville Male's Jason Osborne, and Fairdale's dynamic duo of Carlos Turner and Jermaine Brown stole the spotlight from the lanky swingman.

When Anderson's senior season produced impressive statistics— 24.7 points per game, 9.7 rebounds, and 3.7 assists—Ohio State came calling. The Louisville Cardinals, Anderson's hometown team, sought out players from across the state.

"They went after guys like Tick Rogers," Anderson says. "I mean, no offense to him or other Louisville players, but I was like, 'Are you serious?' I was just hurt. I felt I had done everything that was asked of me, and they still didn't want me. I was a U of L fan to the bone."

Anderson committed to Ohio State and quickly proved himself. He scored more than 500 points in his first two seasons with the Buckeyes; but Ohio State was hit with NCAA sanctions prior to his junior year, and Anderson chose to transfer.

Rick Pitino, who opted not to recruit Anderson two years earlier, had learned from his mistake.

"Growing up in the West End, it wasn't that we hated Kentucky, it was just that you didn't watch Kentucky," Anderson said. "I really didn't know anything about UK. It was all about U of L."

But when Anderson left Ohio State, there were only two programs that drew his interest: UCLA and Kentucky.

"I never paid attention to U of L. It came down to talent, how the teams played, and who I thought could win a national championship," Anderson says. "And I wanted to fit in and help us win."

"We've had a lot of luck with transfers," Pitino told the *Lexington Herald-Leader* in 1996. "All I can say is, thank you Ohio State for giving us Derek Anderson.

# THE SETTING

As a Kentucky Wildcat, Anderson played Louisville at least once a season. The annual UK/U of L basketball face-off is nationally televised and has established itself as one of the biggest—and most heated—college basketball games in the country.

The 1994-95 season was doubly painful for Anderson: Kentucky fell to Louisville, 88-86, and the UCLA team he spurned won the national championship. To cap off a frustrating season, Kentucky was upset by North Carolina in the 1995 NCAA regional finals. A trip to the Final Four was just out of reach.

But during the 1995-96 season, Kentucky posted a record of 34-2, won the SEC, and delivered the school's sixth national title. They also defeated archrival Louisville by 23 points.

"Just a dream, just like a pro team," says Anderson, who sacrificed much of his game for the good of the squad, averaging 9.4 points per contest. "That team was amazing."

---

Derek Anderson grew up a Louisville fan but led Kentucky to a memorable victory over the Cardinals.

And, as the 1996 Wildcats celebrated on the Meadowlands court in New Jersey, several reporters overheard Anderson say one word: "Repeat."

* * *

The following season, the Wildcats were tagged as a rebuilding squad. They had lost four players to the NBA. Their leading scorers and rebounders were gone, and sophomores Ron Mercer and Wayne Turner would have to shoulder much more of the offense and leadership. Again, it seemed as though Anderson had been underestimated and overlooked.

"It was funny, because Ron and I had worked out all summer," Anderson says. "We had roomed together. We knew we played well together. And it seemed like most of the people had picked him to be the leader and everything. But we knew we had something special, that we could both play together."

Both Anderson and Mercer helped Kentucky jump out to a 10-1 record with a pair of 34-point wins over No. 12 Syracuse and No. 8 Indiana. Kentucky won the Great Alaska Shootout and defeated Anderson's former team, Ohio State, 81-65. The Anderson-Mercer pair, which fans had dubbed "Thunder and Lightning," would average nearly 18 points per game each.

"It was going to be that way," Anderson says. "Coach [Pitino] told us in the beginning that we were the scorers on the team, and everyone knew their roles. By the time we played U of L, we had it rolling."

The No.3 Wildcats were ready when it was time to travel down the road to Louisville's Freedom Hall to face the No. 14-ranked Cardinals. And soon, the Cardinals would know the truth about Derek Anderson. They should have recruited him. And they shouldn't have made him angry.

"The day before the game, I was at a mall in Louisville in the East End," Anderson says. "I was there with some of my people, and there, in the middle of the mall, I looked over and I saw [Louisville forward] Nate Johnson with some of his people. So neither of us spoke," Anderson says. "We just kept walking."

Then one of Johnson's friends opened his mouth.

"He said, 'Wait until tomorrow,'" Anderson remembers. "It was like burning fuel for me. I always play better when I'm mad."

# THE GAME OF MY LIFE
## NO. 3 KENTUCKY 74, NO. 16 LOUISVILLE 54
### DECEMBER 31, 1996
**BY DEREK ANDERSON**

I do play better when I'm mad, but when you're mad, you don't enjoy the game as much. I always enjoy when I'm playing, and that's why I smile. But I didn't enjoy that game for a long time.

When I played Louisville my senior year in Freedom Hall, I was mad. I was mad they didn't recruit me, and I wanted to show them why they should have recruited me.

I was at a boiling point when we started that game. Coach told us how good a team they had and how we had to give everything we had to beat them, and that just made me even madder.

We all knew there's no bigger game—other than a championship game—than the U of L game. The first half was really back and forth. Both teams were good, and they played that way in the first half.

I remember I posted up Alvin Sims, then I made a move in front of him and dunked one in. But I remember we just couldn't pull away. Both teams were trying to get into the game.

Then I made The Dunk.

[Anthony] Epps got a loose ball for a runout, and he passed it to me. It was just me and a guy in front of the basket. I don't care who you are, if I get the ball in that situation, I'm going to dunk on you. It just so happened that the guy under the hoop was Nate Johnson.

And I dunked on him—hard. Johnson was called for the foul. That felt good.

\* \* \*

I think we were down a point at the half, and there was so much emotion, there was no talking. We didn't say anything at halftime. We just wanted to get back out there and finish it.

But at the beginning of the second half, there was a moment when someone forced a loose ball, and I grabbed it and shot a fadeaway bank shot that felt real good. Then I hit a three. Then the whole team was on. And by the 10-minute mark, we had stretched the lead to around 20. We knew then the game was over.

For that whole game, I hadn't smiled. I only smiled when Coach took me out of the game with about two minutes to go. I scored about 19 points, and only when I came out did I really enjoy that game.

I finally got my justification. It was personal, and I wanted to do it there in Louisville where all my friends were. That was the most memorable game of my career, other than the national championship.

**Statline:**

| MIN | FG | FGA | FT | FTA | REB | A | ST | PT |
|-----|----|-----|----|----|-----|---|----|----|
| 34 | 8 | 13 | 2 | 4 | 6 | 2 | 2 | 19 |

# THE RESULT

When fans mention The Dunk, some think of James Lee's stuff at the end of the 1978 national championship game. But for a whole new generation of Wildcats fans, The Dunk describes Anderson's high-flying jam on Nate Johnson in the 1997 UK/U of L game. In a photo of the moment, which ran in newspapers the next day, Anderson is positioned nearly parallel to the ground, in an absurdly athletic move, as Johnson struggles to get out of the way. Anderson's face is contorted in anger as he screams.

"I still have a picture of it somewhere in a scrapbook," Anderson says. "That was a big, big moment. Hey—I was mad."

Sadly, Anderson's career at Kentucky would come to an abrupt end just 18 days later. On January 18th, Anderson tore the ligament in his right knee during a game against Auburn. Many predicted the injury would end the star's career.

"It was like my whole world came crumbling down on me," Anderson says. "That moment, it was like everything I wanted went out the door."

Mercer became the leader of the Wildcats that season, averaging more than 18 points per game and earning All-America honors. The offense ran through Mercer in Anderson's absence.

The overachieving Wildcats went on to win 35 games, suffering merely five defeats. They won the SEC Tournament and charged into the Final Four for a second consecutive year.

Meanwhile, Anderson recuperated in record time. He returned to practice by March, just in time for the Wildcats' playoff run. But Pitino refused to play Anderson. If Anderson played and again injured his knee, he would jeopardize his potential professional career. The only way Anderson would take the court, Pitino said, was if technical foul shots needed to be made.

\* \* \*

In the semifinal of the 1997 Final Four, the Wildcats faced a rugged Minnesota team coached by Kentucky native Clem Haskins. As the game slowly turned in Kentucky's favor, Haskins argued with officials, earning a technical foul. Pitino told Anderson to get up.

"That was concentration," Anderson says. "You talk about concentration, that was it." Anderson made both free throws.

"That was history," Anderson says. "I scored, even though I was never technically in the game."

Two days later, the Wildcats fell to Arizona during overtime of the national championship game. Anderson had foreseen back-to-back championships, and his prediction nearly came true.

Many fans were frustrated to see Anderson on the bench. The Big Blue Nation recognized Arizona's advantage, as Arizona's quick guards, Miles Simon and Mike Bibby, constantly beat the Wildcats. The game would have been different, they say, if Pitino had played Anderson.

"I think we'd have won it," Anderson says. "I know Coach Pitino was thinking of me and my career, and it would've been horrible if I'd gotten hurt again. But it was tough sitting there on the bench, man."

# AFTER BLUE

In retrospect, Pitino's decision to confine Anderson to the bench seems wise. After his senior year, Anderson was chosen as a second-team all-SEC performer by the league's coaches. Then he was selected 13th in the first round of the NBA draft by the Cleveland Cavaliers. Anderson had a solid NBA career as a member of seven teams, including Miami Heat's 2006 NBA champions. And, reflecting on his career, he says he harbors only one regret.

"I wish I would've shot more," he says. "Coaches have told me I needed to try and do more, to take over. I wish I'd have shot the ball more. I could always do that."

Nevertheless, things have turned out well for Derek Anderson. "I just never let anybody take my dreams from me," he says.

# CHAPTER 24

# CAMERON MILLS

A Lexington native and life-long Kentucky basketball fan, Cameron Mills wanted nothing more than to follow in the footsteps of his father, Terry Mills, who had played for Adolph Rupp from 1968 to 1971. But that didn't look like an option. Before the beginning of the 1994-95 season, Kentucky was loaded at the guard position.

Tony Delk. Jeff Sheppard. Anthony Epps. Chris Harrison. Allen Edwards. Derek Anderson. Kentucky advised Cameron Mills to go elsewhere.

But during his senior season at Lexington's Paul Dunbar High School, Mills led his team to a second consecutive state tournament runner-up finish. He felt his three-point shooting touch would flourish in Rick Pitino's style. "I held out hope," Mills says. "It was an unfounded hope, but I still held out hope anyway."

Mills began to entertain offers from other schools. Georgia offered Mills a scholarship, and when he floundered, the Bulldogs pressured him to commit. But something kept him from doing it.

"I know what it was," Mills says. "I didn't want to go to Georgia. I wanted to go to Kentucky. But I didn't want to turn down a full scholarship to an SEC school. I had a decision to make."

Terry Mills still had ties to the University of Kentucky—namely, with legendary equipment manager Bill Keightley, who'd held the same position when Terry was a reserve guard. So Cameron's father went to Keightley to make one last pitch on behalf of his son.

When he arrived at Keightley's office—a room known for its vast collection of Kentucky sports memorabilia—then-UK assistant Billy

Donovan was also there. Donovan insisted that UK had no room for another guard.

"That's where the story gets fuzzy," Mills says. "I don't know who suggested it—my dad, Coach Donovan, Mr. Keightley, or Coach Pitino—but somehow, it came up that I could walk on if I wanted to play there so badly."

And so, Cameron Mills committed to walk on at UK.

# THE SETTING

Although Mills received very little playing time during his freshman season, he watched and practiced with a talented Kentucky team that reached the NCAA regional final. During his sophomore year, seniors Tony Delk, Walter McCarty, and Mark Pope led the Wildcats to their sixth national championship.

He participated on Kentucky's junior varsity squad with other little-used players, including Nazr Mohammed and Oliver Simmons. And by the time Mills earned a scholarship in 1997, he had developed into a deadly shooting guard—a weapon to be brought off the bench when offense was needed.

Mills played an even more important role when senior guard Derek Anderson suffered a career-ending injury early in the conference schedule. "That was a magical run for me," Mills says. "I was shooting the ball at meaningful times like I never had before."

Sophomores Scott Padgett and All-American Ron Mercer shouldered the scoring load for the Wildcats, and Mills came off the bench to help lead the team in another run to the title game. He connected on 10 of 16 threes in the SEC tournament and hit for an amazing 63 percent of his three-point attempts during the NCAA tournament. The Wildcats' season came up just short of back-to-back national titles, as they lost in overtime to Arizona, 84-79. Mills scored 12 points.

Then came the fallout. Mercer left for the NBA. Anderson, now fully healed, was no longer eligible. Point guard Anthony Epps graduated. And coach Rick Pitino bolted for the NBA as well, accepting a position with the Boston Celtics.

---

Cameron Mills started his career as a walk-on, but he developed into one of the deadliest shooters in the country.

New coach Tubby Smith was hired immediately. He was a Pitino disciple and former Kentucky assistant coach, and the fans seemed to agree with the selection. But no one knew what to make of the remaining players.

The good news: senior Jeff Sheppard, who had sat out the previous season, was back and ready to lead the team. Transfer Heshimu Evans was eligible. Scott Padgett and senior Allen Edwards could help pick up the scoring load, and juniors Wayne Turner and Nazr Mohammed had developed into quality players.

But for Mills, that summer was one of relaxation. "I had embraced success," Mills says. "I didn't really do anything that summer to improve my game. I worked out, but I didn't do the things I should have to make myself better. And that came back to bite me."

When the 1997-98 season began, Mills found himself in a different place than he had previously known. "I was now the first or second person off the bench, coming in for serious minutes," he says. "But I wasn't scoring, I wasn't making shots. Even in practice, I wasn't making shots. I didn't know what was wrong."

It was a shooter's worst nightmare. Mills was in a slump. And the only way to get through it was to keep shooting. But there were flashes of brilliance. In a 75-72 win over Indiana, Mills came into the game to hit four consecutive three-pointers. "It felt good to make a difference again," he says.

Still, the team as a whole had a difficult time adjusting to Coach Smith's newly implemented system. This was not a run-and-gun, pressing squad like Pitino's teams. This was a team that could score on the perimeter, but also on the inside. It could out-rebound most opponents and lure big men into defending taller players outside the paint. It would work inside-out. It would play half-court offense and defense. And this team would win.

Fans puzzled after an early-season blowout loss to No. 1 Arizona. They fretted after a close loss to rival Louisville. But that game seemed to right the Cats, who reeled off nine consecutive wins—eight over conference foes—before heading into a nationally-televised game against Florida.

Although the Gators were unranked, the matchup made for a good headline, as they were coached by Billy Donovan, another former Pitino disciple. The Gators also featured hotshot transfer guard Jason Williams. And although Williams and fellow Gator guard Kenyan Weaks had huge games, one player would outscore them all. The player Kentucky didn't need: Cameron Mills.

"I was frustrated because I just wasn't producing, and I wasn't helping the team very much," Mills says. "But this day, Dick Vitale and Brent Musburger were doing the television commentary for the game. I couldn't remember Brent Musburger doing one of my games before. I mean, this is Brent Musburger, you know?"

Mills, Vitale, and Musburger walked on to the Rupp Arena court a few minutes before Kentucky tipped off against the Gators. Vitale introduced Mills and Musburger, and asked the young basketball star about his less-than-impressive season: "Cam—what's going on?" Mills remembers Vitale asking. "You're not getting a whole lot of clock these days."

"The team doesn't need me right now," Mills responded.

Vitale would repeat the story on air many times throughout the game. The Wildcats needed Cameron Mills on February 1.

# THE GAME OF MY LIFE
## FLORIDA 86, NO. 7 KENTUCKY 78
### FEBRUARY 1, 1998
### BY CAMERON MILLS

Well, we started out and we were just playing an awful game. And because I really wasn't shooting the ball all that well, there really wasn't any indication I'd come out and do what I did.

Then all of the sudden—you hear players say they're in the zone?—well I was in the zone.

I think Jeff Sheppard got into some foul trouble early in that game, so I came in for him with a lot of time left in the first half. My first shot was different for me. I never drove to the basket. But we were rotating the ball around, and my defender went for the steal. He missed it, so I took the ball and drove to the right side, and I hit a 14-foot bank shot.

On another trip down, I got the ball down low and put it in and got fouled. That was a three-point play. Then I started hitting threes. I started coming off screens that my teammates were setting for me, and the shots starting going in.

When I hit my third three of the half, I ran back down court, and I teared up a little bit. I was so frustrated with how I just hadn't been able to produce. I had been getting time, and I didn't feel like I was helping very much. Then all of a sudden, here's my shot again.

Still, Florida was putting on a show. Jason Williams and Meaks were hitting all kinds of shots, and we weren't playing very good defense. I don't think that it was because they were better than us; it's that we were playing so bad. I know we were down by as much as 15 in the first half, but we had cut it down [to six] by halftime.

Coach Smith wasn't happy. And there was definitely no attitude like 'If it weren't for Cameron, we wouldn't be in this game.' The entire halftime was spent focusing on playing better. A lot of time was spent on how we were going to stop Jason Williams.

I don't remember thinking about how many points I had during the course of the game. But there was a time when I knew I was really in that zone people talk about. My first three of the second half, I pump-faked at the top of the key. At the moment of release I knew it was off. I took off to follow my shot because I knew it had missed, but when I got in the lane, it had swooshed through the net.

Throughout the game, we never played that much better. We just couldn't get over the hump. And after I hit a three late in the game, we called timeout. We walked over to the bench, and I looked up at the score. At Rupp, when you score, they flash your number and your point total up on the screen. So I looked up and saw my number 21, and by that I saw a 28. I had 28 points. I was like, 'Are you serious?'

Of course, the problem with all of this is we lost the game.

## Statline:

| FG | FGA | 3FG | 3FGA | FT | FTA | PTS |
|----|-----|-----|------|----|-----|-----|
| 10 | 19  | 8   | 14   | 3  | 3   | 31  |

# THE RESULT

The 86-78 loss to the Gators exposed a number of the Wildcats' weaknesses—namely, perimeter defense. Although Mills had the game of his life, dropping in eight three-pointers, it went for naught, as the Gators hit 12 of their own. Only one other Wildcat—Padgett—scored in double figures with 10 points.

"After the game, Florida made some comments about how they knew they were going to beat us," Mills says. "So we changed some things. We changed the way we warmed up. We really focused more on defense. We were not as good of a team as we should have been. And this was one of the games that helped prove that to us. So we worked harder."

And the Wildcats' efforts showed. Kentucky lost once more—to

Mississippi—before reeling off 13 consecutive wins to bring home their seventh national title.

During that run, Mills made his presence known again. He didn't make his first field goal until the regional final against Duke. But when Heshimu Evans deflected a rebound out to the top of the key with 2:15 to play, Mills was there to sink the three, giving Kentucky its first lead. The basket capped off a comeback that saw a 16-point Duke lead erased in nine minutes, and Kentucky advanced to a third-consecutive Final Four.

Mills then hit two clutch three-pointers in the second half of the national title game against Utah. His first three tied the game at 58 with 7:46 left, and his second cut the Utes' lead to one, 64-63, with 5:32 left.

But, Mills says, it was the game against Florida that brought back his shot.

# AFTER BLUE

"I never scored that much, ever—in high school or middle school," says Mills, who is now a full-time minister and part-time community educator. "That was special."

Today Mills travels the state with Cameron Mills Ministries, Inc., raising money for the ministry and speaking to students and others about the joys of leading a Christian life. He represents Compassion International and Christianspeakers.com.

He is known for showing audiences his 1998 championship ring and throwing it to a member of the crowd, discarding it as if it were just another dimestore trinket. He tells his listeners that his championship ring means little in life. It is his experiences, he says, that matter, along with his relationship with the Lord.

"That's what it's really all about," Mills says. "Your walk with the Lord is the most important thing. I have been truly blessed."

# CHAPTER 25

# ALLEN EDWARDS

It seemed natural for Allen Edwards to play college basketball in the Sunshine State. His brother, Doug, starred at Florida State, and his other brother, Steve, was a starter for Miami. But Allen would go his own way, carve his own path. He would make a name for himself at the University of Kentucky.

"Everywhere I turned, either coach [Billy] Donovan or coach [Rick] Pitino were there," says Edwards. "I knew I wanted to go away from home, and at the time, I developed a nice relationship with Coach Donovan. I felt like Kentucky was the place I needed to be.

As a 6-foot-5 point guard at Miami's Senior High School, Edwards was a prized recruit. He had learned the game from his brothers and was a smart, athletic player who could score.

But coming to Kentucky in 1994 wasn't easy. The lineup was littered with the names of college basketball's elite: Delk, Rhodes, McCarty, Epps, Prickett, Ford. Playing time was hard to come by.

"It was difficult to break into that group," Edwards says. "We were so good. Those teams were so talented. You really had to be patient and wait your turn."

As it happened, Edwards would get his chance to shine a little earlier than expected. But nothing could prepare him for his senior year, a season that would prove how much Kentucky needed Allen Edwards—and how much Allen Edwards needed UK.

# THE SETTING

Edwards' first season at UK produced 28 wins, SEC regular-season and tournament championships, and one missed opportunity: a loss to North Carolina for a spot in the Final Four.

As a sophomore, Edwards was a bit player for what many considered to be college basketball's No. 1 team. Tony Delk, Anthony Epps, Walter McCarty, Antoine Walker, Mark Pope, and Jeff Sheppard, among others, helped reel off an amazing string of victories.

"The firepower from that team could come from anywhere," Edwards says. "We could score from the outside and the inside. We could run you to death. We were amazing."

Over the course of 17 games, the Wildcats suffered just one loss to No. 1 UMass, and their average margin of victory in conference games hovered around 20 points. Although there were some tough games early on, few teams came close to challenging Kentucky—with the exception of Tubby Smith's unranked Georgia Bulldogs.

On January 24, 1996, in a steamy gym in Athens, Georgia, Tubby's team pushed the seemingly unbeatable Wildcats to the limit.

Enter Allen Edwards, who did not even make an appearance in the game until late in the second half. Edwards seemed fearless, paying no mind to the stressful environment or the situation. He scored two crucial buckets late in the game to help eek out an 82-77 win. It would prove to be Kentucky's closest game of the season. The Wildcats went undefeated in the SEC, thanks in part to Edwards' heady play, before going on to defeat UMass and win the school's sixth national title, 76-67, over Syracuse.

Edwards finally got his shot in 1997. Fellow guard Jeff Sheppard had red-shirted due to an excess of talent on the team. But early in the conference season, senior sensation Derek Anderson injured his knee. Anderson was sidelined for the year, and the Wildcats needed Allen Edwards.

Edwards averaged 8.6 points per game before misfortune interfered yet again. He fractured his right ankle in the SEC Tournament championship victory against Georgia. Consequently, he could play only six minutes in the overtime national title game loss to Arizona.

---

Allen Edwards provided senior leadership on the road to the Wildcats seventh national title, but nothing could make up for the loss of his mother during the season.

* * *

Between Edwards' sophomore and junior seasons, his mother, Laura Mae, was diagnosed with breast cancer. By the time her son was a Kentucky senior, few realized how bad her condition was—including Allen.

Edwards' final season at UK ushered in a number of changes. The talented Kentucky team was ready to make another run at the championship under newly appointed head coach Tubby Smith.

Allen Edwards began the season with a fury, but by the winter months, it became clear that basketball was far from his mind. He scored in double figures in 10 of the team's first 16 games, but he averaged just five points over the next 10 contests.

Laura Mae was unable to attend the beloved senior day festivities. By that time, she was far too ill. Instead, Allen's sister, as well as his brother, Doug, came in his honor.

On the basketball court, Kentucky raced to a 26-4 record. On February 25, 1998, No. 7 Kentucky beat Auburn, 83-58 to clinch the regular-season SEC championship—Edwards' third SEC title since he'd arrived in Lexington.

A day later, he learned that his mother had passed away in her home in Miami. In the midst of a thrilling victory, Tubby Smith drove Allen Edwards to the airport so he could attend Laura Mae's wake. "We had such a big high, winning the SEC," Smith later told *Sports Illustrated*. "But getting this news just tore our hearts out."

Smith told Edwards to come back when he was ready. While he was gone, Kentucky continued on its path of destruction, bound for the SEC Tournament finals. Jeff Sheppard had evolved into a terrific leader and reliable scorer, constantly running off screens to spot up and drain three-pointers or mid-range jumpers. At just under 14 points per game, he'd become the team's leading scorer.

After learning of his mother's death, Edwards spent three days in Miami with his family before returning to play in the first round of the SEC Tournament. He scored six points in a win over Alabama.

In the SEC Tournament semifinal, Kentucky faced 16th-ranked Arkansas. This time they would play without Edwards, who was attending his mother's funeral in her hometown of Holly Hill, South Carolina. Fueled by the emotion of the Edwards family's loss, Kentucky easily defeated the Razorbacks, 99-74. But Sheppard was injured badly during the contest, limping off the court in the first half with a sprained left ankle. He would be unable to play in the championship game against South Carolina the following day.

After the funeral, Edwards returned to the team and stepped up his game. He would play defense on South Carolina's dangerous guard, B.J. McKie. He would become a leader in Sheppard's absence. And most importantly, Edwards would compensate for the loss of Sheppard's offensive contributions.

# THE GAME OF MY LIFE
### SEC TOURNAMENT CHAMPIONSHIP:
### NO. 7 KENTUCKY 86, NO. 15 SOUTH CAROLINA 56
### MARCH 8, 1998
### BY ALLEN EDWARDS

We left the night of the funeral and got in Atlanta really late. Then we had to get up and go through a shootaround. All the coaches, the trainers, everyone there wanted to sympathize with me. They were all great.

I remember at the pregame shootaround, B.J. McKie and [another South Carolina guard] Melvin Watson both came over to me and said how sorry they were to hear about my mother. Then they wished me the best. It showed great character on their part, and it showed that the game went deeper than the competition. It's about the relationships you have with people. They were extending their hands to help me deal with my life situations. That was very cool. Now when the ball went up, we were battling. But beforehand, to put all that aside, was very heartwarming.

To be honest, that game seemed special from that moment on out. I felt like my mother's presence watched over us in that game, and throughout the rest of that season.

For our team, that year was a year of doubt for a lot of people. We'd lost some guys; we'd gotten a new coach. Could we still be that good? And in the South Carolina game, we'd lost our leading scorer. How would we do?

We came out and just played really well. Like we did all year, that team played together, unselfishly. It was the most unselfish team I'd ever been a part of. We showed how much more of a team we were. Without Jeff, we showed we could still go out there and play.

I wasn't really overcome with emotion because I didn't feel the full effect of my mom passing until the end of the season. I knew it had happened, but I wasn't dealing with it yet.

During the course of the game, we came out hot, and I remember guys in the game just kept telling me to shoot. But I just wasn't that type of guy. We wanted to get everybody involved. We were Kentucky, you know? We were always confident that we were going to beat you.

Against South Carolina, we came out of the gate really fast. We led early, and everyone was getting involved. It seemed like everyone was hitting threes, and we led by [10] at the half. Then we came out in the second half and went on [an 18-7] run that really seemed to put it away.

There was a lot of emotion in that game. I just wanted to help get everybody involved and, ultimately, win that game. But we ended up scoring the last [15] points to win it going away.

It was a real satisfying feeling to bring home another SEC Tourney championship. I knew my mom was there. She knew we'd won.

## Statline:

| MIN | FG | FGA | FT | FTA | REB | A | S | PTS |
|-----|-----|-----|-----|-----|-----|-----|-----|-----|
| 28 | 3 | 7 | 7 | 8 | 3 | 5 | 3 | 15 |

# THE RESULT

Edwards finished the game with 15 points, five assists, three rebounds, and three steals. His defense on McKie was stellar, and the outstanding guard duo of McKie and Watson finished with just 20 points combined.

As Edwards said, the win was a total team effort: Turner scored 18 points, Heshimu Evans added 11 points, Padgett scored nine points, and Mohammed chipped in eight points.

Kentucky hit 13 three-pointers, their highest number of the season; and even walk-on Steve Masiello was able to get into the act, scoring five points and hitting a three. "You got the feeling it was over in the first half," Edwards says.

The run in the SEC Tournament allowed Kentucky to earn a No. 2 seed in the NCAA Tournament's South Region, allowing for the possibility of a matchup with No. 1 seed Duke. Jeff Sheppard recuperated, and Edwards and the other Wildcats veterans were playing well together. Kentucky was confident.

"Early in that season, [center] Jamaal Magloire predicted we'd win the national championship," Edwards says. "Now that's a heavy prediction, but that's the kind of mindset we had." And Edwards was on a personal roll.

When he came to practice that Monday, he noticed that his good friend Scott Padgett had decorated his basketball shoes with a special message: R.I.P. L.M.E. Rest in Peace, Laura Mae Edwards.

"I think what brought the team together most was Allen Edwards' mother's illness and then her death," Tubby Smith told *Sports Illustrated*. "The kids saw the pain Allen was going through. They all said, 'What can we do for Allen?'"

Edwards was touched. "Everyone on that team really cared about one another," he says. "Chemistry was a big part of why that team succeeded."

\* \* \*

In the NCAA Tournament, Edwards continued his streak. He scored 17 points in a second-round win over St. Louis, 10 points in a victory over UCLA in the Sweet Sixteen, and 11 points apiece in thrilling wins over Duke and Stanford to reach the title game.

"In the Duke game, you just felt like you could do nothing wrong," he says of the 17-point comeback in the game's last 11 minutes. "We were hustling and really playing well, and in the last parts of the second half we just felt it was our day."

Sheppard's monster game against Stanford led the Wildcats into the finals against Utah, and after a second-half comeback, Kentucky brought home championship No. 7. Edwards scored four points in the contest, ending his career with a victory.

"Winning the national championship with that team was so special," he says. "We just felt like we were going to do it. Everyone was unselfish and knew what they could do."

# AFTER BLUE

Afterward, Edwards tried his hand at professional basketball. After stints in the Continental Basketball Association and the International Basketball Association, he decided to return to Kentucky in 2002 and complete his degree in sociology.

"Obviously, there were guys I played with who had better individual careers in professional basketball," Edwards says. "But I wouldn't change my decision for anything. I would still go to the University of Kentucky."

After graduating, Edwards pursued a career in coaching. For three seasons, he was a part of Kyle Macy's staff at Morehead State. After a coaching change at Morehead, he left for Virginia Commonwealth.

His goal, he says, is to be a head coach. "I've learned under some great coaches," he says. "I really want to one day give it a try."

He and his wife, LaTanya Edwards, have a six-year-old daughter, Mai'a. Family, it seems, is still the most important aspect of Edwards' life. And over the course of his senior season at Kentucky, his basketball family helped him endure his tragic loss. Along the way, he became one of the most decorated players in Wildcats history.

"I look back on that season a lot," he says. "It was an amazing time."

# CHAPTER 26

# SCOTT PADGETT

There are iconic moments in Kentucky basketball history that can be denoted by a single word. "The Dunk", for instance, brings to mind the image of James Lee sealing the Wildcats' fifth national title in 1978. The Tip conjures memories of Jeff Brassow reaching back and guiding a Rodrick Rhodes' miss through the hoop for a win over Arizona in the Maui Classic in 1993. The Stomp summons recollections of the day when arch villain Christian Laettner trampled Aminu Timberlake in 1992.

Maybe Scott Padgett's shot should be known as "The Three". But there were so many big shots, so many crucial moments, in just one contest. In the minds of Kentucky fans, this game has become known as "The Revenge Game", or simply, "The Greatest Game".

Whatever the nickname, most of the fans who witnessed this game—and its counterpart six years prior—say it was one of the most satisfying Kentucky wins in the 100-plus years the sport has been played in Lexington. And that's saying a lot.

\* \* \*

Scott Padgett grew up as a Kentucky fan in a town divided between those who rooted for the Wildcats and those who were loyal to the hometown Louisville Cardinals. Cardinals fans have always looked grudgingly upon Louisville residents who cheer for the Big Blue.

But during Padgett's childhood, UK was, in a word, fun. Lexington boasted a flashy coach, a fearless style of play, and big-time recruits. The nation had once again begun to realize that Kentucky basketball was king and played an entertaining game.

For Padgett, a gangly forward with big ears and a bigger smile, playing anywhere in college would be wonderful. Recruiting analyst Bob Gibbons rated Padgett as the 121st-ranked player in the nation, and teams like Florida, Florida State, and Purdue were interested.

But Padgett wanted to play at Kentucky. And when Rick Pitino felt his offense could use a 6-foot-9 forward who could sink the three, he called Padgett.

Padgett's personal road to the Final Four would be filled with stumbling blocks. As a freshman, Padgett found it difficult to adjust to college life, especially in regard to academics. He found it even more difficult to crack the starting lineup.

Kentucky was two years removed from the Final Four and a No. 1 recruiting class. Lexington brimmed with basketball talent, and Pitino was trying to mold his first national champion. Padgett wasn't an immediate part of the plan. He averaged just four minutes per game.

"I had my struggles," Padgett says in retrospect. "I partied too much. I didn't go to class nearly enough. I wasn't a great student."

Padgett flunked two classes after his freshman season. That year, UK posted a record of 28-5 and fell one win short of the Final Four. But Padgett was off the team and deemed ineligible for the 1995-96 season due to academic probation. "It was the toughest thing I'd ever had to do," he says.

Scott Padgett went home to Louisville, where he worked as a landscaper, a telemarketer, and a sporting goods salesman for the fall semester. In the spring, Pitino said Padgett could return to the team if he earned a 3.0 grade-point average. Padgett earned a 3.6.

But he still couldn't play basketball. And later that season, when the 1996 Kentucky Wildcats won their sixth national title, Padgett was watching the game from a friend's living room.

"I knew I was growing up, and I would have a chance," Padgett says. "It was hard to watch, but I knew I would be able to help the team after I'd grown up. That was what I had to do."

Just one season later, in 1997, Kentucky basketball was back in the Final Four, led by All-American Ron Mercer, Derek Anderson,

---

Scott Padgett watched Duke defeat Kentucky in the 1992 NCAA Tournament, but six years later, he helped the Wildcats get revenge.

and Scott Padgett, who contributed 9.6 points per game and was named to the All-Final Four team. Kentucky lost the title game in overtime, but the experience was invaluable for Padgett and the Wildcats.

# THE SETTING

Padgett remembers watching the Wildcats play Duke in 1992. He remembers the back and forth, the David-and-Goliath-like matchup. He remembers rooting for Kentucky, the underdogs. Kentucky was going to pull off the stunner against the nation's No. 1 ranked team.

It was over now—Padgett was sure of it. Sean Woods had just hit a running one-handed bankshot over Christian Laettner to give Kentucky a one-point lead.

Yes.

Then Grant Hill threw the pass.

No.

Laettner caught it.

Oh no.

He hit the shot!

"I couldn't believe it," Padgett says. "I was just in shock."

In 1997-98, Kentucky was a new team. Rick Pitino was gone, as were team leaders Anderson, Mercer, and Epps. A new coach, new faces, and a new system were in place, and the changes were, at first, tough to handle.

Wins over nationally ranked Clemson, Purdue, and Georgia Tech offset a tough loss to archrival Louisville; but a 15-point drubbing at the hands of No. 1 Arizona—to whom Kentucky had recently lost the 1997 National Championship—proved just how far the Wildcats had to go to compete on the national stage.

Aside from losses to Florida and 18th-ranked Ole Miss, Kentucky began to gel, utilizing their new personnel and Tubby Smith's ball-line defensive schemes to outscore and out-defend their opponents.

When it was time for the NCAA Tournament, the Wildcats were well prepared. Kentucky had a 29-4 record, an SEC Tournament championship, and loads of momentum. "We felt like we were playing some of the best basketball in the nation," Padgett says.

\* \* \*

In 1994, the NCAA selection committee placed Kentucky and Duke in the same regional, which could have yielded a sequel to the great 1992 contest in the regional finals. But Kentucky didn't hold up its end of the bargain, losing to Marquette in a second-round game. In 1997, Kentucky could have faced Duke in the Maui Invitational Tournament. Again, Kentucky lost to Arizona, preventing the game from happening.

But in 1998, the Cats would get their chance. Third-ranked Duke was the South Region's No. 1 seed, while Kentucky, ranked No. 5, was the No. 2 seed. Neither team had a problem advancing to the regional finals. Kentucky dispatched South Carolina State, St. Louis, and UCLA by 15, 27, and 26 points, respectively.

Duke, led by standout players Trajan Langdon, Chris Carrawell, Roshown McLeod, Elton Brand, William Avery, Shane Battier, and Steve Wojciechowski, was one of the more feared teams in America. With a record of 32-3, the Blue Devils had defeated their opponents by more than 25 points per game.

For Scott Padgett and Lexington native Cameron Mills, playing the Blue Devils was particularly meaningful. "For Kentucky kids who saw Duke beat Kentucky in 1992, it did mean more to us," Padgett says. "We wanted to beat them so bad. It was life and death for us, beating Duke."

# THE GAME OF MY LIFE
## NCAA REGIONAL FINALS:
## NO. 5 KENTUCKY 86, NO. 3 DUKE 84
## MARCH 22, 1998
### BY SCOTT PADGETT

This game has to be talked about, even though it isn't my best game, personally. That's all it was about when we were in school was winning. But it wasn't easy against Duke.

In the beginning of the game, they were doing anything they wanted to against us. They were hitting shots; they were rebounding. They couldn't do anything wrong, and we couldn't do anything right. But we wanted to win so bad; I think we were too excited.

We went into halftime, and we were down by, I don't know—a lot [10 points]. But in the locker room, Tubby said, 'We're going to win this game.' And he kept saying that, even through the rest of the game.

Even in the second half, when they came out and started scoring more points, we still didn't talk about getting the game close. We talked about winning it. We never thought we weren't going to win. I remember we kept talking about how we had to keep chipping away to win. We wanted to take it one possession at a time to come back.

But then things started to look worse. We were down by 17 with about 11 minutes to go; and right then, when it was looking the worst, that's when we started to come back. The play after we went down 17, I believe we hit a couple threes—I hit one—to cut it to 14, and then 11, and then it was like, 'Alright now, let's go.'

That's when Wayne took over the game. Our point guard, Wayne Turner, knew he was quicker than anyone on Duke's team, and he knew his penetration could break them down. So he started to go to the hole.

A lot of us made shots, but he took over the game. They couldn't stop him one on one. So we started running a lot of pick-and-rolls for him to get into the lane, and he hit some big buckets; but he was also was just finding everybody on the outside. During that run, they couldn't call a timeout.

Earlier in the half, they called their last timeout on a loose ball. It actually should have been called a jump ball way before they called timeout, but the referees gave them the timeout. But it was their last one, and man did it work out great for us. You know, when we were making that run, it's one of those situations when if you have a time-out, you want to use it, but they didn't have one.

And it seemed like for us, it was one of those times when the game just couldn't stop. Even when there was supposed to be TV timeouts and things like that, there weren't, because there was no stoppage of play. We just kept going up and down the court.

It seemed like we were just lucking out. We'd get a steal, or they'd miss, and we'd keep scoring. For eight or nine minutes, we played with no stoppages.

In my mind, the three plays I remember most are Wayne's drive where he beat their guard to the hole, and the ball ran around the rim and fell in, and he was fouled. Then he pumped his fist. The lead was down [to eight].

Then we had fought back to within two points, and we had one of our few bad shots of the entire run. Someone shot a bad three, but Heshimu Evans made a great tip-out, right to Cameron [Mills'] hands. If you're on the other team and the ball comes out to Cameron and he's wide open, you're in trouble. That's not what you want to see.

And he hit the three to take the lead.

That's when we felt like we'd done it. Everybody was pumped. We thought they wouldn't be able to come back then.

But they fought back to tie it at 81, and with about 30 seconds left, Wayne and I ran the high pick-and-roll at the top of the key. He'd been killing them all day, so I set the screen, and there was so much penetration, Elton Brand went to help on Wayne in the paint. So when Brand went over, I had a wide-open three.

Wayne got it to me and I let it go; and when it went through, I went running back to the other end of the court yelling. I was screaming, "We got this!"

### Statline:

| MIN | FG | FGA | 3FG | 3FGA | REB | PTS |
|-----|----|----|----|----|----|----|
| 38 | 4 | 10 | 3 | 5 | 6 | 12 |

# THE RESULT

Kentucky had closed a 17-point margin in 11 minutes against one of the nation's best teams. The prize: a trip to the Final Four.

But Duke had one last shot. In 1992, Kentucky held a one-point lead over Duke with 2.1 seconds left for the Blue Devils to make a miracle play. In 1998, Kentucky held a two-point lead over Duke with 4.5 seconds left.

But there was one big difference. In 1992, Grant Hill threw a perfect pass to Laettner, who drained an open shot. Six years later, Tubby Smith elected to guard the inbounds man—something Pitino decided against in 1992. Duke was forced to inbound the ball to Avery far in the backcourt, giving him one option: to dribble as far upcourt as possible and take a wild half-court shot. The ball fell harmlessly away—into Padgett's waiting arms.

"When it left his hands, it was pretty straight, so I knew it had a chance," Padgett says. "But then I saw it coming off, and I was able to reach up and get it."

But Padgett didn't have the ball for long. "I still, to this day, kick myself," Padgett says. "I got the rebound on that play, and I should own that ball right now. But after I rebounded it, I threw it up in the air. To this day, I wish I still had that ball."

Instead, team captain Jeff Sheppard, who scored 18 points and grabbed 11 rebounds, snatched the ball.

"That game is one I'll always remember," Sheppard says. "That's one of those that you always like to say you were able to be a part of."

"Kentucky has great kids," coach Mike Krzyzewski told *The New York Times* afterward. "They have amazing camaraderie. This is a loss that hurts."

Nearly all of Duke's players performed well. McLeod finished with 19 points and eight rebounds. Carrawell scored 12 points. Wojciechowski scored 10 points and had four assists. Langdon scored 18 points with five rebounds. Battier chipped in 11 points and eight boards.

But for all of Duke's fire in the first half—including 54.8 percent shooting—the Blue Devils went cold in the second, shooting just 33.3 percent. Duke was also outrebounded, 45-39.

It's rare that a game equals the endless hype provided by cable television, the reporters, and the fans. But the Duke-Kentucky rematch was the Godfather II of basketball games—the sequel that matched the original.

It was "A victory that provided payback," said Thomas George of *The New York Times*.

"We're going to treasure this moment for a long time," Tubby Smith told *The Times* after the game. "I'm sure our fans and players feel that they have been exonerated."

It was true. "It felt like we'd done something for the state, for all UK fans," Padgett says.

\* \* \*

Led by Sheppard, Edwards, Turner, and Padgett, the 1998 Comeback Cats finished 35-4 and won their seventh national title in San Antonio, defeating Stanford and Utah in the Final Four.

"Winning a championship is always what it's all about at Kentucky," Padgett says. "We were able to do what a lot of teams only dream of."

Padgett again made the All-Final Four team. And, after missing out on the 1996 championship, Padgett finally had his title.

And Padgett returned to defend the championship, accompanied by fellow seniors Turner and Evans. In what many deemed a rebuilding season, the Wildcats finished 28-9, winning the SEC Tournament title.

Padgett ignited the Wildcats' spark in a second-round NCAA game when 14th-ranked UK met 22nd-ranked Kansas in New

Orleans for a spot in the Sweet Sixteen. Down five with 1:09 remaining, two Turner free throws and a Padgett three-pointer tied it up in regulation. Kentucky won in overtime, 92-88, thanks in large part to Padgett's 29 points and 10 rebounds. "Probably my biggest shot and individual game," Padgett says.

Kentucky looked to be on the way to an improbable fourth consecutive Final Four when the Wildcats were upended by second-ranked Michigan State, 73-66.

"We tried to teach the others how to step up and carry on the tradition," Padgett says. "But it was tough because we knew our time was finished."

# AFTER BLUE

Padgett was chosen No. 28 in the first round of 1999 NBA Draft by Utah, where he established himself as a big man who could step outside and shoot the three. He parlayed his career at Utah into free agent signings with Houston and New Jersey.

The one-time college flunkie has become an NBA millionaire. Padgett married his college sweetheart, Cynthia Dozier, and the couple has two sons and a daughter. "It's fun, it really is," Padgett says. "I've had a lot of success, and I'm lucky."

And there's a perk to playing with the Houston Rockets, his latest team: he gets to throw salt on former-Blue Devil Shane Battier's wounds. "It's great having one of those Dukies on my team," Padgett says, laughing. "He hears about that game a lot."

# CHAPTER 27

# JEFF SHEPPARD

The teacher asked each sixth-grader whom he or she would trade places with for a day, and Jeff Sheppard didn't even have to think about it.

"I said I wanted to be Larry Bird," he says. "But only if I could go to Kentucky and win the national championship first."

Even Sheppard seems a bit mystified when he is asked how he became such an avid Kentucky basketball fan. For children growing up in Peachtree City, Georgia, there was only one sport—football. And there was only one team—the beloved Georgia Bulldogs.

But there were clues indicating that Jeff Sheppard was destined to play for UK. Friends of the Sheppard family were fans of the Big Blue, and Sheppard took easily to basketball. He attended Kentucky basketball camps as a child. And a player named Rex Chapman captured his interest. Sheppard wanted to emulate Chapman's high-flying game.

Throughout high school, Sheppard desperately wanted to play basketball in college—and if he was good enough, he wanted to play for Kentucky.

But first, he had to get noticed. He was chosen as a third alternate for a Georgia All-Star game. When the other alternates were unable to attend, Sheppard accepted the invite and made the most of his opportunity.

He wowed the crowd with his leaping ability, winning the dunk contest and attracting the attention of Kentucky assistant coach Herb Sendek. Sendek mentioned Sheppard to then-Kentucky coach Rick Pitino, who began to recruit the McIntosh player.

But Pitino had one concern—could Sheppard shoot the three consistently enough to be a factor in Kentucky's system?

Sheppard's coach Steve Hale invited Pitino down for a look. "I called up some guys and we got a pickup game going," Hale told *Sports Illustrated*. "It was one of the first times I told Jeff to shoot jumpers exclusively, and he made a lot of them."

Pitino didn't need to see anymore. Sheppard was going to be a Wildcat.

# THE SETTING

Jeff Sheppard quickly realized that he would need to get much better if he were going to make his mark at Kentucky. As a senior, he earned *Parade* All-America honors, but during his first workout with the Wildcats—an intense weight room session—Sheppard vomited in physical exhaustion.

The previous season, Kentucky had signed the nation's No.1 recruiting class, won 30 games, and advanced to the Final Four. Pitino had a solid group of returning athletes, and Sheppard only saw mop-up time as a freshman, averaging just under four points per game.

But as a sophomore, he broke into the lineup, starting 27 games and scoring 8.3 points per game. Pitino named him the team's Most Improved Player. But another great recruiting class almost sunk Sheppard's career.

With talented transfer Derek Anderson in the fold, as well as incoming McDonald's All-Americans Ron Mercer and Wayne Turner, Sheppard's playing time grew thin. But it was hard to complain, Sheppard says, being a member of the 1996 Wildcats, who won 34 games and came away with the school's sixth national title.

"We were so talented, it was all about doing what you could for the team," Sheppard says. He did his part, shooting 50 percent from the three-point line. Pitino gave Sheppard the team's sacrifice award.

But in the 1996-97 season, Pitino re-evaluated the lineup. The point guard positions were filled by Epps and Turner. Mercer and Anderson, along with Allen Edwards, Cameron Mills, and Scott

---

Jeff Sheppard grew up idolizing Rex Chapman, but Sheppard did something King Rex never did: Sheppard won two national championships.

Padgett would fill the off-guard and small forward spots. Where did Sheppard fit in? On the bench, Pitino said. Sheppard agreed and opted to redshirt. He practiced with the team but warmed the bench during games in hopes of playing the following season.

Little did he know, Anderson would injure his knee early in the conference schedule and end his Kentucky career. As a result, Kentucky lacked team quickness. After a masterful run to a second consecutive Final Four, the Wildcats lost the national title to Arizona in overtime, 84-79. Sheppard's athleticism would've been invaluable in the championship game.

The day after the loss, the returning team selected Sheppard as their captain. But he would have to wait until his senior year to get back on the court.

* * *

By the time Sheppard returned, Anderson, Mercer, and head coach Rick Pitino had left for the NBA. Senior Jared Prickett had graduated. Tubby Smith replaced Pitino, and Smith's first campaign did not begin smoothly. Although the team started the season 10-2, the losses hurt. The Wildcats appeared outmatched in a 15-point loss to the same Arizona team that defeated Kentucky in the title game the previous year. The other loss—a three-point defeat at home to unranked Louisville—was shocking.

It became clear to most Kentucky fans that the 1997-98 Kentucky squad would not be challenging for another Final Four. But those fans were in for a surprise. The team finished the year with 19 wins in 21 games and captured SEC Tournament and regular-season championships.

Sheppard led the way, earning a spot on the league's All-SEC third team after averaging 13.7 points per game. Center Nazr Mohammed established himself as a solid scorer and rebounder, while Padgett continued to improve. Turner continued his outstanding play at point guard.

The Wildcats proved they could win games in lots of ways, with quick guards and big, thick centers and forwards. Players like Padgett and Heshimu Evans could bang down low and step outside to hit the long-range jumper.

But Sheppard carried the team. And despite injuring his ankle in the SEC Tournament—which the Wildcats would go on to win without him— Sheppard was ready for the NCAA Tournament a week later.

Kentucky, a No. 2 seed in the South Regional, made quick work of unranked South Carolina State and St. Louis in the NCAA Tournament before dispatching an injury-plagued UCLA team, 94-68.

Sheppard was huge in the comeback win over No.1 seed Duke in the regional finals. That sent the Comeback Cats—as CBS referred to them—to the Final Four for the third consecutive season.

The nation was surprised when Kentucky advanced, yet again, to the Final Four. But their opponent, tenth-ranked Stanford, was perhaps an even more shocking competitor in the NCAA Tournament. The Stanford players would prove themselves on the court. But unfortunately for the Cardinal, they didn't have Jeff Sheppard.

# THE GAME OF MY LIFE
## NCAA NATIONAL SEMIFINAL:
### NO. 5 KENTUCKY 86, NO. 10 STANFORD 85
### MARCH 28, 1998
**BY JEFF SHEPPARD**

We had three great games in a row where we came back to win and get that championship. But to me, the Stanford game sticks out. It was so unique the way we were able to make comebacks the way we did, over and over. We had the ability of putting team goals before the individual goals. We were 17 down against Duke, 12 down against Stanford, and 10 down against Utah—and we came back each time. We just kept playing together.

The win over Duke was so big, and I hear that a lot because it meant so much to Kentucky fans. But then we had to come back and play again.

In the Stanford game, we just wanted to keep our momentum going. After all, we had a lot of experience in the NCAA Tournament. We knew what it was like to be in the Final Four. So we were just trying to keep that attitude, keep winning.

The whole atmosphere of the Final Four—that's the biggest thing to handle. But we were used to it. We didn't get wide-eyed and overzealous. That was because our goal wasn't to get to the Final Four; our goal was to win the national championship.

We'd seen Stanford on tape, and we knew they were big, physical; we knew they could shoot the ball. It was scary; they were the same as us. So we knew we had our work cut out for us.

They had had some emotional games in the tournament, too,

with a comeback of their own, so they were really similar to our team. So we trusted our coaches to put together the best scouting report they could.

Still, you have to play the game. When we came out, they jumped on us early [11-3]. We always knew we were going to make our run, but it was tough because we were fouling so much and sending them to the free throw line. We felt we were the better-conditioned team, though, and we felt that at some point, they would break.

We came back a little at the half [down 37-32], but it seemed like we could've closed the gap a little more if any of us could've hit any shots. We didn't really hit very well from three in that first half [1 for 9].

At halftime, I don't remember folks screaming and yelling a lot. The half was more of a strategic plan, where we were making small changes, talking about plays we needed to run more. That was the way I ended up scoring a lot of points. We set screens, and I came off those screens, and that's what we did. It was that curl play. We kept calling the curl, and I just kept hitting buckets to keep us in the game. But Stanford did as well.

Nazr came up big in the second half and had a monster game [17 points], and then our press started to take over. We got some turnovers, and after being down 10, we were back in the game real quick.

For the last 10 minutes, it seemed like one team would make a shot and lead by a point, then the other team would take the lead. I think I hit a couple of threes with a few minutes to go, with that curl, and we were up by four points.

But then [Stanford guard Arthur Lee] tied up the game with a three, and we went into overtime. We both scored a few times, and then, with [1:30] to go, Scott [Padgett] went in and missed a dunk. The ball went out of bounds, but we got the ball back, and Coach drew up the curl. So I came off the screen, caught it and shot. And that one went in, too. I was in a great rhythm.

I remember we were up a point and they had a chance to heave it from past half-court, so they did—but it wasn't close.

Afterward, we were all just tired, but we knew we were going to play for the national title.

## Statline:

| MIN | FG | FGA | 3FG | 3FGA | REB | A | PTS |
|-----|-----|-----|-----|------|-----|---|-----|
| 33 | 9 | 15 | 4 | 8 | 6 | 4 | 27 |

# THE RESULT

Sheppard finished with a career-high 27 points, helping to overcome Lee's 26 points and five assists. For Stanford, guard Kris Weems scored 17 points, and forward Mark Madsen scored nine points and grabbed 16 rebounds.

For Kentucky, it was another team effort. Edwards had 11 points, Padgett scored 10 points, Mohammed scored 18 points, and Turner finished with eight points.

After a day off, Kentucky played in its third consecutive national title game against Utah, a team the Wildcats had faced multiple times in the tournament throughout the 1990s.

"It didn't matter if we had to turn around and play the next night," Sheppard says. "We had to get ready." But part of the fun, he says, was enjoying the experience. "You do have to consciously think about that," he says. "It all goes by pretty quick, so you want to enjoy every step along the way. It helps you focus, too."

Since 1993, Kentucky had faced Utah in three NCAA Tournaments: 1993, 1996, and 1997. In each, the Wildcats ended the Utes' season by 21, 31, and 13 points, respectively.

It could be surmised that Utah head coach Rick Majerus was worried when he heard he would again face the Wildcats—this time for the title.

The game went as predicted. Utah, with its stellar guard Andre Miller and big, versatile front court, led early, and took a 10-point lead into halftime.

As the saying goes, the Wildcats had them right where they wanted them. The Comeback Cats made one final stand. A Mills three-pointer with less than eight minutes to go finally tied the game. A second later, a Sheppard steal and dunk gave Kentucky the lead. The Utes were slowly running out of gas.

But after one final run put them ahead by four points, another Mills three-pointer and a Sheppard shot from the baseline secured Kentucky's lead. Over the final six minutes, the tired Utah squad would score only one field goal, and the Wildcats continued to run away, winning 78-69.

In Tubby Smith's first season as head coach and Jeff Sheppard's last season as a Wildcat, Kentucky won its seventh national title. Sheppard scored 16 points on his way to being named the Final Four's Most Outstanding Player.

# AFTER BLUE

"I'm just so blessed," Sheppard says. "Very few people get to live out their dreams."

Sheppard played one season in the NBA with his hometown Atlanta Hawks, where he appeared in 18 games and averaged 2.2 points. He then played professionally in Italy for three years.

But family brought him back home. He married Stacey Reed, who played basketball for the women's team at Kentucky, and together, they have a little girl, Madison. Living in America with his family is more important than playing basketball overseas, he says.

Now he sells sports merchandise through his own company, 15inc. And he always hears about his heroic games.

"Kentucky basketball is common ground for anybody in the state," Sheppard says. "It was a real blessing to be able to be a part of the Kentucky program, to represent the state. I'm still living out the dream, whenever anybody asks me about the games."

# CHAPTER 28

# TAYSHAUN PRINCE

Ever since coaches began watching Tayshaun Prince play basketball, they all told him the same thing:

"Gain some weight."

"You're too skinny."

"How do you expect to make the NBA with those rail-thin arms and those matchstick legs?"

They had a point. But at 6-foot-7 and 180 pounds, the kid could shoot. It was a weird, left-handed shot that seemingly took off too late from his palm. But the ball went in the hoop. And he had range, too. But how would this skinny high schooler get off his shot against bigger and stronger players?

Surprisingly, Prince would use his lack of girth as a weapon. And he would eventually silence his high school critics. After winning a state championship as a junior, it seemed Tayshaun was on the radar of every major college. Most recruiters loved his shooting touch, and at 6-foot-9 (after an adolescent growth spurt), Prince's long wingspan could be utilized for great defense.

As a senior, Prince was named a McDonald's All-American. He won the prestigious *Los Angeles Times* George Yardley Award, given to the best player in Southern California. Other winners included Baron Davis and Paul Pierce. He had his choice of colleges. Prince says he was recruited by all the major programs—all except one.

"North Carolina," he says. "They never sent me anything."

# THE SETTING

Prince committed to Kentucky, which was coming off a second national championship in three seasons and would need to replace some of its scoring.

Tubby Smith immediately utilized Prince, starting him in 11 games during his freshman season. The UK team was led by its seniors, Wayne Turner, Scott Padgett, and Heshimu Evans, among others. After a run to the elite eight, the Wildcats lost to second-ranked Michigan State, 73-66, concluding a three-year streak of NCAA title game appearances.

UK would become Prince's team the very next season. He averaged 13.3 points per game and was named second-team All-SEC. And Prince would become known as one of the most clutch players of the Tubby Smith era.

During Prince's sophomore season, Kentucky entered the NCAA Tournament with a 22-9 record and a share of the SEC regular-season title. Nineteenth-ranked Kentucky earned a five seed and faced 12th-seeded St. Bonaventure in the first round.

The game was much tougher than anyone could've anticipated. With seven seconds left, Kentucky trailed 63-60, until Prince drained a three-pointer to send the game into overtime. Kentucky led by three with time dwindling when the Wildcats fouled a St. Bonaventure guard on a three-point shot. Three free throws later, the game went into a second overtime.

But Kentucky finally pulled away, 85-80. Prince scored 28 points.

That Kentucky team, widely perceived as an underachieving bunch with a lack of chemistry, lost in the next round to 16th-ranked Syracuse, 52-50.

As a junior, Prince produced one of the finest seasons Kentucky fans had ever seen. He averaged 16.9 points, 6.5 rebounds, and was named an All-American and SEC Player of the Year. That season, his two free throws helped UK defeat Louisville, a floater in the lane won a game over South Carolina, and a baby hook with 3.3 seconds left gave the Wildcats a 71-70 win over Florida in Rupp Arena.

In the NCAAs, Prince scored 27 points in a surprisingly close 72-68 win over former UK assistant Ralph Willard's Holy Cross squad in

---

Tayshaun Prince was always told to gain weight and change the form on his jumpshot. Luckily, he never did, and he developed into an All-American.

a first-round game. Then, with 31 points from Prince, No. 9 UK was able to defeat No. 24 Iowa, 92-79. Still, the efforts were insufficient in returning Kentucky to the Final Four, as the 24-10 Wildcats were upset by unranked Southern California, 80-76.

And the future didn't look too good. Prince announced his decision to test the waters in the NBA Draft.

* * *

NCAA rules state a player can attend workouts to gauge his possible draft status, but the player must apply or withdraw his name from the draft by a certain date. Tayshaun Prince and teammate Keith Bogans decided to see where they stood with the NBA scouts.

After workouts and pre-draft camps, scouts were whispering, yet again, about Prince's ability. At just over 200 pounds, how could Prince get his shot in the NBA?

In college, Prince utilized his size and quickness. If a bigger defender came out to guard him, he would pump-fake and go to the basket. If a small guard tried to stop him, Prince would post him up on a low block. Most of the time, either situation generated points. As a junior, the forward shot 49.5 percent from the field and 84 percent from the free-throw line.

But in the NBA, the basketball world grew bigger, tougher, and quicker. Guards could range from 6-foot-4 to 6-foot-9. Small forwards could be 7 feet tall.

Prince and Bogans followed the experts' recommendation. They returned to Kentucky to continue their college careers.

As a senior, Prince averaged 17.5 points and 6.4 rebounds. And in the unlikely event that someone in the basketball world hadn't yet heard of Tayshaun Prince, they would after his senior faceoff against North Carolina.

# THE GAME OF MY LIFE
## NO. 11 KENTUCKY 79, NORTH CAROLINA 59
### DECEMBER 8, 2001
#### BY TAYSHAUN PRINCE

There are a few games that stand out to me. St. Bonaventure was a great game for me. Some others stand out, like when I scored 41 against Tulsa. But North Carolina at home was big. If I had to pick,

I'd pick that one.

That game was at home, it was at our building, and I gave the fans something they won't forget.

Florida was our rival at the time, and believe it or not, so was Tennessee, with Tony Harris and those guys. They had some problems, but they were really good. But Carolina was big for us too.

When we played them, that game had two great teams with great traditions. It was made for TV.

I was never—NEVER—as hot as I was to start that North Carolina game. I came out and I hit my first two threes and they weren't anything spectacular. Both of them were at the top of the key. On the third one, I was a little deeper, and [North Carolina's Jason Capel] was on me. But I made that one, too. The fourth one, I thought I might as well keep shooting, so I made a move, and I had a guy on me, so I dribbled and stepped back behind the line and let it go. I felt really good when that one went in.

So that was the first 12 points of the game, and the next time down, they were looking for me to shoot it. I don't have a clue how far out I was when I shot it, but I knew they were going to get a defender on me, so when I came across half court, I was going to shoot. Some people said it was from the 'K' on the court logo [27 feet].

The reason I took it is because I'd made four straight. When I got the ball again, there I was. So I put it up and it went in. That crowd went crazy, and I could see the North Carolina players were just like, 'Oh, man.'

That was our first 15 points. And then, we never looked back. Like I said, I've never been that hot.

For one, I haven't had the opportunity to do it again. That was the right time and the right place to do it, because for one, the guys believed in me to take those type of shots at that time. You know, for me to be able to be the No. 1 option on the team, I could come out and I had the green light to go and score. Like I said, it was the perfect time to do it.

But the one thing I remember about the game besides the three-pointers is how we really shared the basketball.

I always remember [UK guard] Rashaad Carruth was on the team at that time, and whenever he was in the game, I always tried to find him all the time, because he was—believe it or not—he was a lot better three-point shooter than I was. So I always tried to look for him, and I did a few times. He'd knock down shots, and he knocked down a few in that game.

We had great all-around play in that game, so it's always going to be a memorable game, besides the three-pointers.

At halftime, I remember thinking, "This is a game I'm going to remember for a long time." For one, I'd remember it just because of the fans and the way they acted. They were so loud and pumped up. For two, I just loved seeing the joyous looks on my teammates' faces at the time.

When I saw that, and we won and everybody was so happy, I knew that game would be No. 1 in my memory.

### Statline:

| MIN | FG | FGA | 3FG | 3FGA | REB | A | S | PTS |
|-----|----|-----|-----|------|-----|---|---|-----|
| 35 | 11 | 22 | 7 | 11 | 11 | 4 | 4 | 31 |

# THE RESULT

Prince made North Carolina pay. The coaches from the only team that did not recruit Tayshaun Prince were undoubtedly wishing the lanky forward was a Tar Heel that day.

In a matchup of two legendary basketball programs, Kentucky defeated a depleted North Carolina squad 79-59 for the 1,800th win in school history. Prince dropped in 31 points, but none were more memorable than his first five shots—all three-pointers, all good—and none more outrageous than his 27-foot bomb.

"I've never seen anything like that in all my days of basketball," Tubby Smith told Jeff Drummond, of the Big Blue Den Web site. "[Prince] was just possessed. His radar and where he was shooting them from were just unbelievable."

North Carolina's Capel agreed. "I just have to congratulate him," he told Drummond. "He shot the ball great today."

Only one other UK player finished the game in double figures—Marvin Stone, who had 11 points. But eight other Wildcats scored at least four points.

Prince's fourth three-pointer gave Kentucky a permanent lead at 12-10. The Wildcats improved to 5-1 on the season while North Carolina fell to 1-4.

\* \* \*

But Prince saved his best game for the NCAA Tournament. At 20-9, the fourth-seeded Wildcats defeated Valparaiso in the NCAA first round in St. Louis before meeting Tubby Smith's old school, 12th-seeded Tulsa, in the second round.

In 37 minutes, Tayshaun Prince scored a career-high 41 points, including six of eight from behind the three-point line—one of which came from a few steps behind the arc merely seconds before the first half ended.

The performance was reminiscent of another left-handed shooter who wore number 21 and scored 41 points for UK in the 1978 tournament final versus Duke—Goose Givens. The Wildcats would need every single Prince point in a hard-earned 87-82 victory.

"[Prince] hit a three that was ridiculously long," Tulsa coach John Phillips told Drummond after the game. "If you make one from 25 feet, it's your night." Evidently, Phillips hadn't seen the tape of the North Carolina game.

But Prince's luck would run out in the very next game, as UK lost to eventual national champion Maryland, 78-68, in the Sweet Sixteen.

For all of his clutch baskets and dominating performances, Prince was unable to play in the Final Four. But by the time his career ended, he had put his name high in the Kentucky record books.

# AFTER BLUE

Joe Dumars of the Detroit Pistons was convinced Prince could play in the NBA, and despite wide-spread doubt regarding Prince's size, he chose the Kentucky star with the 23rd pick in the draft. Dumars liked the way Prince's long wingspan allowed him to play defense on bigger and smaller players.

After five seasons in the NBA, Prince has proven to be a find. He became a starter during his second season and won a world championship in 2004. He is a remarkable scorer, averaging 12.1 points for his career; and his reputation as a clutch player continues with a 12.4 scoring average in 80 career playoff games.

In 2004, as the Pistons made their run to the championship, Tayshaun Prince executed an iconic play, hustling back to block a Reggie Miller layup in Game 2 of the Eastern Conference Finals. The Pistons won the game and the series. They went on to defeat the Los Angeles Lakers in five games.

Prince became the new face of Kentucky basketball in the NBA. He was a star without being a star—a hardworking, defensive-minded opportunist. Now, Prince says he is living his dream.

"The thing about living a dream like this, when you were as hungry as I was as a kid about getting to the NBA, there was nothing else that was going to stop me from getting here," Prince says after a game against the Indianapolis Pacers. "You always hear about great talents that never make it, or—because of different obstacles they face in life—they don't overcome. Guys in this league, all around this league, have had obstacles, just like everyone. But some find ways to get through it. Some don't let anything stop their goal. I'm just one of those guys that didn't let anything stop me."

And Kentucky was a big part of that, he says. "Every game, to go out with that crowd, was great," he says. "I loved it all, all my four years. It helped me get to where I am today—living the dream."

## CHAPTER 29

# PATRICK SPARKS

Patrick Sparks did not grow up like other rural Kentucky kids—he was not a big Kentucky basketball fan. As a boy, Sparks' heart belonged on a soccer pitch. "I played soccer all the way through high school," Sparks says. "I think it was always my best sport, really."

His home life was divided between his mother's residence in Tennessee and his father's place in Central City, Kentucky. He did not identify with other Kentuckians' passion for the basketball team, simply because he was not always in the state.

As a teenager, Sparks chose to attend high school in Central City, the home of The Everley Brothers music group. Years later, the city would also become known as the hometown of a Kentucky basketball legend—Patrick Sparks.

Sparks lettered in basketball, soccer, and cross-country during high school. But as a basketball player, Sparks showed uncanny quickness and vision. He also developed a long-range jumpshot, enabling him to connect from well beyond the traditional college three-point line. His talents led his team to the state tournament—and he was getting noticed, too.

Division I programs took note of his impressive statistics. As a senior, he led the state in scoring with 31.4 points per game. But in the end, two schools vied for his skills: Auburn and Western Kentucky. Both colleges began recruiting Sparks early in his high school career.

The University of Kentucky, however, did not offer a scholarship. Head coach Tubby Smith told Sparks he could walk on to the UK team. Sparks said thanks, but no thanks.

Sparks felt he fit in well with the Hilltopper team and Western Kentucky coach Dennis Felton. In 2001, the Hilltoppers were a mid-major team on the rise, coming off an NCAA Tournament appearance, a Sun Belt Conference championship, and an upset win at Louisville over Denny Crum's Cardinals. Felton had recruited Chris Marcus, a 7-foot-tall project from North Carolina, and surrounded him with talented, athletic role players. The team was in a position to defend its conference title and return to the NCAA Tournament.

After Sparks committed to WKU, the fans on campus were excited. Felton had the program going in the right direction. Many believed Sparks was another diamond-in-the-rough recruit who would make a difference. Felton said as much in a conversation with a friend that year: "If I didn't get him, it would have set me back four years."

# THE SETTING

It was well known in Lexington and Bowling Green that Kentucky did not openly want to play Western Kentucky. And it made sense. Kentucky had nothing to gain from the matchup. If the Wildcats won, it was because they were supposed to—but it would not look good if they lost.

Still, before the 2001 season, Kentucky agreed to play WKU in a small four-team tournament at Rupp Arena. It did not go well for the Wildcats. Loaded with talent, Tubby Smith's fourth-ranked Wildcats boasted future pros Tayshaun Prince, Keith Bogans, and Gerald Fitch. WKU's roster included Marcus, as well as Kentuckians Derek Robinson and Mike Wells.

The game, close throughout the first 30 minutes, blew open late. In some cases, WKU proved to be more athletic, with more consistent shooters who likely wanted to win more than the Wildcats. In the end, the Hilltoppers celebrated a 64-52 victory. The last play featured freshman Patrick Sparks, who stole the ball from Prince, the Kentucky player who would eventually be named an All-American.

After the Kentucky game, the soft-spoken Sparks said he couldn't be happier with how his college career began. "This is unbelievable,"

---

Patrick Sparks left Western Kentucky to sink clutch shots for the Big Blue at Kentucky.

he said in the locker room. "To come out and beat Kentucky, it just means so much to all of us. I don't know what to say really."

By mid-season, Patrick Sparks was a starter. The Hilltoppers quickly established themselves as the class of the Sun Belt, assembling another 20-plus win season. Despite an outstanding regular-season record, the Hilltoppers would need to win their conference tournament to receive a bid to the NCAAs. So with just seconds remaining in a tight game against New Mexico State in the 2002 Sun Belt Tournament semifinals, the responsibility fell on freshman Patrick Sparks.

Trailing 72-71, Sparks took the inbounds pass, pump-faked his defender, took a dribble, and launched a 19-footer that fell through the net for the win. A day later, WKU won its second consecutive conference tournament for another NCAA bid.

A week later, Sparks played well beyond his years, pouring in 20 points and dishing nine assists against Stanford in a first-round NCAA Tournament loss.

During his sophomore season, Sparks became an all-conference point guard, averaging 13.6 points and 5.9 assists. He led his team to yet another NCAA Tournament birth as MVP of the conference tournament. Things were going quite well in Bowling Green. But a controversy in Athens, Georgia, changed the lives of everyone involved.

Jim Harrick, the former coach of the UCLA Bruins who had left amid allegations of improper recruiting, had worked his way back to the world of elite coaching at Georgia. But the familiar allegations resumed, and soon, Harrick was forced to leave the school.

After WKU's resurgence, Dennis Felton had quickly become a hot commodity in the coaching world, and Felton was trying hard to get the Georgia job. After the 2003 season, WKU fans heard the dreaded news: Felton was leaving for Georgia.

But would the players leave, too? Yes, one player left. And unfortunately for those in Bowling Green, it was WKU's best: Patrick Sparks.

Sparks had formed a bond with Dennis Felton, but he did not want to follow him to Georgia. Other schools had noticed the talented Central City boy, and they came calling. The University of Louisville, now coached by former Kentucky head man Rick Pitino, wanted Sparks. And so did Mike Montgomery and Stanford. Lastly, Sparks got a call from Tubby Smith.

"I never was a die-hard Kentucky fan," Sparks says. "I just wanted to go to the place where I could get the best education."

Still, there's something special about a Kentucky boy playing for his home-state school. Tubby Smith had realized his recruiting mistake, and he got Patrick Sparks the second time around.

\* \* \*

After coaching underachieving Kentucky squads in 2001 and 2002, Tubby Smith put together a fabulous run in 2003 and 2004. And with leaders Chuck Hayes and Kelenna Azubuike, as well as an outstanding group of incoming freshmen, Sparks found himself on an exceptionally strong team with a chance of advancing to the Final Four.

After posting a 6-1 record, ninth-ranked Kentucky entered its annual rivalry game with 13th-ranked Louisville looking to prove itself as an elite team. The Cardinals had defeated the Wildcats two years in a row. And Pitino's Louisville squad had a few stars of its own: All-American Francisco Garcia, shooting guard Taquan Dean, and Louisville-born swingman Larry O'Bannon.

What followed was one of the most controversial and thrilling game endings in the 25-plus years of the competition.

# THE GAME OF MY LIFE
## NO. 9 KENTUCKY 60, NO. 13 LOUISVILLE 58
### DECEMBER 18, 2004
### BY PATRICK SPARKS

We started off terrible in that game. It felt like we couldn't hit any shots. And [Louisville] played really, really good. They were doing what they do, hitting shots, running up and down the floor. We couldn't do anything.

At halftime, we just kept talking about how we needed to get back in to the game. We were down [32-16], and it felt like we hadn't even started playing yet.

We just needed somebody who could start hitting shots. So we came in the second half, and, lucky for us, I just got hot. It's when you get in that zone. You just start to feel like everything's going in. So then other guys—Ravi [Moss] and Kelenna—hit some shots, and [Louisville] started missing. Our defense picked up, and in just a few minutes, we'd played our way back into the game. But it all led up to that last play.

Playing Louisville is always the biggest game of the year at Kentucky. That's the one you always want to win. So yeah, everyone always wants to win that one the most. And it does seem bigger if you're from Kentucky, even though I didn't really grow up in Kentucky my whole childhood. I grew up in Tennessee, too, but for other guys from Kentucky, you could tell how much it meant to them.

So we came back to take the lead by one, but [Garcia] hit a shot in the lane, so they took the lead again. We had a play to run, but it wasn't working, so I called timeout [with just under five seconds left].

The next play we called worked like it was supposed to. I threw the ball in to Kelenna, and they double-teamed him, so I was open in the corner. He got the ball back to me, and I saw [Louisville forward Ellis Myles] coming at me, so I pumped and got him up in the air so that he fouled me.

On the free-throw line, I knew we were down one, and I had three shots. Then they called timeout, so I had some time to think about it. But then Coach called me over and we started talking. He asked me a weird question, like 'Where are you going for Christmas?' And I said I was going home. That's all he really said.

Then I just stepped up and I put them in.

**Statline:**

| MIN | FG | FGA | 3FG | 3FGA | REB | A | PTS |
|---|---|---|---|---|---|---|---|
| 32 | 8 | 15 | 5 | 8 | 5 | 3 | 25 |

# THE RESULT

"I knew he'd make them," Kentucky forward Chuck Hayes told the *Kentucky Sports Report* after the game. "There is no other guy we'd rather have on the line."

Kentucky capped off its biggest comeback in 12 years when Sparks hit the game-winning free throws. The Wildcats led for just six minutes, but the team got hot when it mattered most.

"We did things that championship teams do," Smith told the *Kentucky Sports Report*. "I thought our guys didn't panic; they kept their poise and we did the things we needed to do to win."

The Cardinals dominated the inside in the first half, forcing UK's guards into woeful 5-for-24 shooting; but the game turned in the second half when freshman forward Juan Palacios left the court with an eye injury.

Kentucky inserted a smaller, more experienced lineup, which drove into the lane and kicked out to shooters for open jump shots. At one point, Sparks scored 12 points just to keep Kentucky in the game.

But with 11 minutes to play, Kentucky was still down 46-30. A crucial 14-2 Kentucky run brought the Wildcats back into the game. Sparks hit a three and then created a traditional three-point play, which was followed up with a Moss three and two Azubuike free throws. With 1:27 to go, UK was in the lead.

Sparks capped the game of his life with the final play, earning the foul and hitting all three free throws with six-tenths of a second remaining. For the first time in three years, Kentucky had beaten Louisville in the most dramatic way possible.

Later, Cardinals fans claimed that Sparks had traveled before his shot attempt, and video evidence showed there was a shuffle of the feet. But it didn't matter—victory belonged to the Wildcats.

Sparks hit five three-pointers and chipped in five rebounds and three assists to go along with his 25 points. Azubuike scored 12 points, while Hayes scored six points and grabbed nine rebounds. 20,088 fans witnessed the game—a Freedom Hall record crowd. But only the Big Blue faithful went home happy.

Sparks' stepmother, Michelle, saw the game in person, but his father, Steve, was traveling with the Muhlenberg North team in London, Kentucky, more than two and a half hours away. Michelle held up her cell phone so that Steve could hear what was going on in the game while he watched on TV from his hotel room.

"It's the old kid-in-the-backyard, game-on-the-line kind of thing," Steve Sparks told ESPN's Pat Forde after the game. "It's a classic. You'll hear kids talk about it all the time."

\* \* \*

During his eighth game, Sparks earned his place in Kentucky history. Many had forgotten he'd defeated the Wildcats in his first college game. But Sparks' legend continued to grow. The guard's big-game heroics always surfaced when his team needed him the most. Later in the season, Sparks hit seven three-pointers to defeat Alabama in Tuscaloosa and win the SEC regular-season championship.

And in the final game of the season, his 20 points and rim-dancing three-pointer at the buzzer sent the Wildcats into overtime with Michigan State for a trip to the Final Four. Although the Wildcats fell to MSU, they finished the season 28-6.

Sparks' senior season featured more big shots—but an overall decrease of talent in Lexington led to a disappointing 22-13 record.

But Sparks saved his personal-best game for last. Vastly out-manned talent-wise in an NCAA Tournament second-round matchup against second-ranked Connecticut, Sparks poured in 28 points to keep his team in the game. But Kentucky fell, 87-83.

# AFTER BLUE

Sparks left Kentucky after playing just two seasons for the Wildcats, but his knack for making clutch shots made him a fan favorite.

During a postseason barnstorming tour, Sparks and his fellow seniors traveled to towns across the state, playing various all-star teams. And Sparks showed how good he really was. He scored 62 points in one appearance, 100 in another. The fans loved it.

"It's a good time coming out and playing for the fans," Sparks said after his 62-point effort. "This is what it's about. Just coming out and having fun."

# CHAPTER 30

# RAJON RONDO

Contrary to popular belief, Rajon Rondo has always had ties to Kentucky basketball. He's always been friends with Derek Anderson Jr., whose father starred with the Wildcats in 1996. "Oh yeah, Rajon's like another son to me," Anderson says.

But Rondo's road to becoming a Wildcat was one mired in controversy and—as some thought—luck. Rondo says it wasn't as controversial as it seemed.

College coaches loved Rajon Rondo ever since they first laid eyes on the high schooler with the huge hands and even bigger wingspan. He could pick off passes and take them to the other end for quick scores. And he could play defense. Oh, how he could play the man-to-man defense.

As a junior at Louisville Eastern High School, Rondo became an All-State performer. It was then, he says, he got a scholarship offer. "Louisville offered me after my junior year," Rondo says. "But it was too early for me, so I said I wanted to wait."

Rondo also wanted to wait because he knew the Cardinals were interested in another point guard: New York City legend Sebastian Telfair, whom Cards coach Rick Pitino openly courted. Telfair was the latest great New York player—a cat-quick guard who, like Rondo, could run an offense and play defense. But unlike Rondo, who had a questionable outside shot, Telfair could shoot the three consistently. Pitino was hooked, and Telfair was equally enamored. The New York guard committed to the Cardinals.

But many experts, including those from ESPN, predicted Telfair would never set foot on Louisville's campus. They said he would leave for the NBA and bypass college altogether. Pitino's gamble was justified. Never before had a player under 6-foot-6 inches tall bypassed college and been selected in the NBA's first round.

While Pitino waited for Telfair, Rondo opened up his recruitment. He went to Oak Hill Academy's basketball factory in Virginia for his senior season, where he became a McDonald's All-American. "I went away for my senior year and I was able to show people what I could do against the best high school players," Rondo says.

Tubby Smith offered Rondo a scholarship, and in the spring of 2004, he signed with UK. "I'd gone away for high school, so I wanted to stay close to home for college," Rondo says. "I wanted my Mom to be able to see me play. It wasn't because I wanted to get back at U of L or anything like that. UK was just the best place for me to go."

Telfair would eventually submit his name for the NBA Draft and forego his college eligibility. He was drafted by the Portland Trailblazers in the first round, and he even signed a multimillion-dollar shoe contract.

Louisville did not get their man, and they also didn't get Rajon Rondo. Pitino later said that his handling of the Rondo-Telfair situation was one of the biggest recruiting mistakes he has ever made.

* * *

Rondo's contributions to the Kentucky program began months before he set foot on UK's campus. He assisted with recruiting, convincing Detroit guard Joe Crawford and Atlanta forward Randolph Morris to commit to the Wildcats. Both players were also named McDonald's All-Americans and the trio, along with New York guard Ramel Bradley, became the No. 1 recruiting class in the nation. Joining the freshmen was Central City guard Patrick Sparks. The fans expected the 2004-05 Wildcats to be a competitive bunch.

As a freshman, Rondo started as the team's point guard. The team went 28-6, with a sterling 14-2 mark in the SEC—good enough for the regular-season league championship. The Wildcats fell just short of the Final Four, losing a grueling double-overtime game to Michigan State.

# THE SETTING

That's when the drama began. Randolph Morris declared for the

Rajon Rondo chose Kentucky over his hometown Louisville Cardinals, and he was 2-0 versus the Cards.

NBA Draft. But he wasn't drafted in the first *or* second rounds. He tried to come back to school but had to serve a suspension. And after senior Chuck Hayes graduated, the Wildcats lacked leadership. It was not an easy transition.

The 2005-06 Wildcats began the season ranked No. 9 in the nation. But they quickly dropped to No. 23 after a 6-3 start that saw Kentucky defeat just one ranked opponent. In its higher-profile games—Iowa, North Carolina, and Indiana—Kentucky did not play well. In fact, on December 10, the Wildcats lost to rival Indiana by 26 points—the most lopsided loss for a Kentucky team in 16 years.

Louisville, in the meantime, had not played many competitive games. And so the Cardinals won them all, coming into the contest with a perfect 6-0 record. They also had not played any away games.

In the week leading up to the Louisville game, Rondo said he spoke with his Louisville high school coach, Doug Bibby, and Tubby Smith. "We talked and both coaches talked about how we needed to run more," Rondo says. "It was good for me and Coach [Smith] to talk. We both knew what we wanted to do against U of L."

On Game Day, 24,432 fans crammed into Rupp Arena—the second-highest number of people to watch a Kentucky game in the arena's 30-year history. The Big Blue nation would love what it saw.

# THE GAME OF MY LIFE
## NO. 23 KENTUCKY 73, NO. 4 LOUISVILLE 61
### DECEMBER 17, 2005
### BY RAJON RONDO

We got busted by 26 against Indiana right before the U of L game. The Cardinals were No. 4 in the country, and we were on CBS. They were undefeated, and we had a chip on our shoulder. That game was our chance to prove something.

I had talked with [Eastern High School] Coach Bibby that week, and we talked about speeding up the game. Coach [Smith] and me talked about the same thing, and I thought it went really well.

Coach [Smith] was real intense those days leading up to the game. I wouldn't say he was angry, but there was definitely no BS-ing around. But we had a good week of practice and, on top of everything else, it was [equipment manager] Bill Keightley's birthday the day of the game. Everybody has a great relationship with him, so we wanted to win even more.

It was a packed gym; more than 24,000 fans were there. Everybody always gets so excited for that game, because everybody knows that other than March Madness, it's the most important game we have. For me, it was bigger than it is for most other people, because it's the game you always hear about during Christmas break. There's always talking between the fans and your friends. And you know most of the guys on the other team, too.

The big thing in that game was that from the tip to the end, Coach let us run. That was big. I was ready for that. I wasn't nervous at all. The first couple of possessions, a lot of people were just settling in. I'd played with some of their guys—[Brandon] Jenkins, [Andre] McGee, and [Taquan] Dean—in the summer. Normally, there would have been some talking going on between us. But they couldn't talk very much in that one—all they had to do was look at the scoreboard.

There was a dunk that Joe Crawford made along the baseline. I threw him a pass and he made a quick move and took it to the basket. That made the crowd go wild.

It seemed like that in the first few minutes, we were already up by about 10. We never looked back. We never trailed. They ended up cutting the lead to two or four, and then I hit a three. Then got a three-point play, and then I fed Shagari [Alleyne] for a dunk.

I went coast to coast a couple of times in the game, but I remember a move I made where I was at the top of the key on the pick and roll. I moved to the basket and got a little finger roll on [Louisville forward] Brian Johnson. That was nice. I had to give him a little look after that.

At halftime, we knew what we had to do. We were up by a lot, but we knew they could come back. Then we came out in the second half and kept running.

The last year [in 2005], they were up big on us, and we came back on them—so we knew not to get a big head. But I never really said very much. That was for [seniors] Pat [Sparks] and Ravi [Moss]. They were the vocal leaders of the team.

But we had a lot of fun in that game. In the second half, we were all excited, and we played like it. It wasn't like the year before, when we fought to come back.

They didn't fight. And I was excited because I could go back home to Louisville over the summer and brag.

### Statline:

| MIN | FG | FGA | FT | FTA | REB | A | ST | PTS |
|-----|----|----|----|-----|-----|---|----|-----|
| 35 | 7 | 12 | 10 | 15 | 3 | 7 | 2 | 25 |

# THE RESULT

The game was never close. Kentucky led 8-0 before Louisville scored. And at one point, Kentucky led by 23 points. The Cardinals missed 13 of their first 14 shots. Rondo contributed his career-high 25 points and seven assists, while junior Sheray Thomas added 11 points and six rebounds. Junior Lukasz Obrzut grabbed nine rebounds.

But for Rondo, the game was more about the home-state rivalry than personal redemption. Even though he wasn't Pitino's point guard, Rondo bares no ill will. "Everybody makes mistakes," he says. "UK was where I wanted to be."

But Rondo's career continued at UK in rollercoaster fashion. He was always a point of controversy. With game-winning shots against

Central Florida (a fadeaway jumper at the buzzer) and South Carolina (a three with under a second remaining), it was obvious the Wildcats needed the talented point guard on the floor.

But he and Coach Smith never saw eye to eye, and confusion replaced cohesion in many of the team's offensive sets. Rondo was even replaced in the starting lineup with senior Brandon Stockton in the middle of the conference schedule. "I'm still happy with my decision," Rondo says. "I had a great time at UK."

Rondo's sophomore season ended with a 22-13 record, 9-7 in the SEC. The team was still in danger of not making the NCAA Tournament when the SEC Tournament began, but wins over Mississippi and Alabama likely clinched the bid—an eighth seed in the East Region.

In the NCAA Tournament, Kentucky gained a measure of revenge in the first round by defeating Alabama-Birmingham, which had beaten UK two years earlier in the tournament.

Kentucky played one of its best games in its last appearance of the season, an 87-83 loss to No. 2 ranked Connecticut. In his last game as a Wildcat, Rondo scored 11 points, grabbed eight rebounds, dished six assists, and committed three turnovers.

# AFTER BLUE

Rondo left Kentucky after his sophomore season. Most NBA analysts gauged Rondo's draft status anywhere from the early teens to the late first round.

After waiting for what seemed like hours, he was drafted No. 21 to the Phoenix Suns. But the Suns then traded Rondo to the Boston Celtics, where he would, ironically, be forced to compete with point guard Sebastian Telfair for playing time. After two years, their paths had finally converged, until Telfair was traded in 2007. It seemed Rondo had beaten out the Boy Wonder from New York for Boston's starting point guard spot.

"You've just got to work hard," Rondo says. "It is a different level, and you have to keep working to keep up." For Rondo, that means developing his outside shot.

But for now, Rondo is getting used to what it's like being a young player in the league. On an off day before the beginning of his rookie season, Rondo is in Lexington, Kentucky, visiting friends. "I just got out of a dance club," Rondo says, although it's 1 p.m. on a

Wednesday. "I've been having fun. But you know, it's cool. You've got to go to work, but you can have fun, too."

After two seasons at UK, it seems Rondo is finally where he wants to be.

# CHAPTER 31

# PATRICK PATTERSON

It was the coach from Texas that finally convinced Patrick Patterson he should come to Kentucky. There was Duke, but Patterson reportedly said he just "wasn't feeling those guys," and Florida, but Patterson wanted his parents to be able to watch him play.

The McDonald's All-American from Huntington, West Virginia, chose the basketball powerhouse in his backyard—the University of Kentucky—instead.

The Wildcats had fallen on hard times. Patterson was used to winning in high school. Paired with fellow high school phenom O.J. Mayo as a senior, Patterson won his third consecutive state championship.

Kentucky was not winning enough for its fans or its administration. Coming off a 22-12 season in 2006–07, then-Head Coach Tubby Smith decided to leave after 10 years in Lexington. He settled in Minnesota, but back in Kentucky, everyone wondered who UK Athletic Director Mitch Barnhart would hire as his replacement.

The names were varied, yet all were widely successful. Billy Donovan. Jay Wright. Rick Barnes. Tom Izzo.

Barnhart settled on a guy from Texas—Billy Gillispie, who had rebuilt several programs, including making Texas A & M relevant in basketball once again.

Gillispie said he knew what he was getting into. He said the first thing he had to do was secure the big-time recruits Tubby Smith could not.

His first objective? Secure Patrick Patterson. At 6-foot-8 and 240 pounds, Patterson could have been a five-star recruit based on his raw potential alone. Patterson held a variety of offensive moves, a jump shot out to about 15 feet and to top it off, he was a smart kid with good grades and stable parents.

In short he was a university's dream student-athlete, and Gillispie had to have him. The Texan put on the full-court press to the Patterson family. When he met them he brought a binder, filled with the younger Patterson's future exploits at UK. It detailed games he would win, honors he would earn, and it mapped out just how he would fulfill his dream of playing in the NBA.

The Pattersons were impressed. They liked this Texan. They liked his accent, they liked how he'd overcome hardships and outworked other coaches to get to this elite level, and they liked that he had a plan for Patrick.

Patterson loved the idea of playing for the Big Blue. When he committed to the Wildcats everything seemed perfect.

# THE SETTING

In reality, it was the furthest thing from perfect. In Patterson's freshman season the team underachieved early, losing games to the likes of Gardner-Webb and San Diego. Patterson performed admirably, (averaging 16.4 points, 7.7 rebounds, and more than a block per game) as did senior guards Ramel Bradley and Joe Crawford. When Patterson suffered a stress fracture in his left ankle the season looked bleak.

The team pulled together to make the NCAA Tournament but lost in the first round to Marquette. Patterson watched from the sidelines in a cast.

His sophomore year was even more forgettable, as questionable coaching and decision-making from Gillispie led to UK missing the NCAA Tournament for the first time since 1991. Instead, the Wildcats lost to Notre Dame in the third round of the NIT. Along the way the team dropped another embarrassing game, this time to Virginia Military Institute (111-103), as well as a stinging 19-point defeat at No. 1 North Carolina, and a second straight loss to archrival Louisville. Again, Patterson missed out on a chance to play in the NCAA Tournament.

Enough was enough. The fans, community, administration and players were ready for a change, and after the season Gillispie was fired. He was too rigid in his ways, players would later say. While he was a smart coach, he did not deal with people particularly well, alienating those influential to the program, like donors and former players. And when a player was more suited to a different style of play (not his deliberate method of offense and defense) Gillispie would not bend; it was his way or the highway.

So, for the second time in two years, a coaching search began in Lexington.

This time  there was really only one name on the list. It was a name the administration had avoided before. Too controversial, they said. Too much baggage.

The name was John Calipari.

He had had problems at his previous school, UMass—they had forfeited their Final Four appearance in 1996 because star Marcus Camby had taken money from an agent. But what many people did not know was that after finding out about the violation Calipari turned in Camby himself.

Calipari wanted the UK job. In fact, he wanted it when Tubby Smith left, but he did not receive a phone call from UK. When Gillispie was fired, those within the UK administration convinced Mitch Barnhart and then-UK President Lee Todd to interview Calipari. Since Gillispie had taken over at UK, all Calipari had done was come within a missed three-pointer of a national title at Memphis, where he earned his second National Coach of the Year Award. The UK officials liked what they heard. When Calipari answered all of their questions during a lenghty interview, the pair were convinced they had their man.

Calipari was hired in the spring of 2009 and a new era of UK basketball began. Immediately, the match of Kentucky's tradition and Calipari's recruiting ability created a college basketball monster—Cal brought in the No. 1 ranked recruiting class, signing John Wall, DeMarcus Cousins, Eric Bledsoe, Daniel Orton, and Jon Hood.

The future looked bright. Most analysts felt UK would be back near the top of the national rankings, with a real shot at vying for another national title.

Patrick Patterson had a decision to make.

* * *

Should he stay or should he go? Patterson could have left and taken millions of dollars in the NBA. Star shooter Jodie Meeks did. Gillispie had left. However, Patterson liked college. If he stayed for his junior season he could graduate in three years and play in his first NCAA Tourney game. He may even get a shot to win a national title.

He decided to stay at UK. And boy, did that season get off to a great start. With the abundance of new talent, the Wildcats started off the year 19-0 and assumed the No. 1 ranking for the first time since 2003. One game stood out to Patrick in that run. It was a win over a traditional power on national television.

To Patrick, it was the game that told the country UK was back.

# THE GAME OF MY LIFE
## NO. 5 KENTUCKY 68, NO. 10 NORTH CAROLINA 66
### DECEMBER 5, 2009
**BY PATRICK PATTERSON**

My favorite Kentucky game was when we played North Carolina at home. It was probably because I scored 19 points and 7 rebounds.

People kept talking about North Carolina all year. They had some good players, like Deon Thompson and a young Tyler Zeller. People kept saying we were too young and that we couldn't compete with them and we ended up killing them in the first half (a 28-2 run). I remember we got off to a good start, and eventually we were up by 19 points.

John (Wall) really wanted to win that game, being from North Carolina, and he played really great to start the game. There's a dunk that people still remember that he had in that game, where he swung from the rim. But we were all excited for that game. North Carolina came back in the second half, because they were a good team, but we still won. John hit some free throws at the end to clinch it, and he and DeMarcus (Cousins), Eric (Bledsoe), and I all had good games.

We pretty much just showed the world what Kentucky is about – that we were back.

## Statline:

| IIN | FG | FGA | 3FG | 3FGA | FT | FTA | REB | BLK | STL | PT |
|---|---|---|---|---|---|---|---|---|---|---|
| 37 | 8 | 12 | 1 | 1 | 2 | 2 | 7 | 1 | 1 | 19 |

# THE RESULT

Patterson's junior season would be his last as a Kentucky Wildcat. And it almost turned out exactly as he wanted it to.

Kentucky's first season under Calipari went like this: A 32-2 record entering the NCAA Tournament, a No. 1 seed, an SEC regular season and tournament championship, All-America honors for Cousins and Wall (second-team All-America honors for Patterson) and a real chance to win UK's eighth national title. The Wildcats certainly looked the part, winning their first three NCAA Tourney games by 29, 30, and 17 points.

But life isn't a storybook, and in a dreadful shooting performance, Kentucky fell to sixth-ranked West Virginia, led by Bob Huggins, 73-66 in the regional finals. There would be no Final Four for Kentucky in

2010. Patterson's collegiate career was over. Afterward in the locker room, many of the UK players left their jerseys on, stunned that they had lost.

One of the greatest runs in UK basketball history was over – and many of the players who made it possible were not going to be back.

# AFTER BLUE

The team's accomplishments in 2009-10 cannot be overstated. In one season, Calipari and his No. 1 ranked recruiting class took Kentucky from the ashes of a failed regime back to the top of the mountain—and Patterson was a huge part of that. He was a leader. But, as Meeks had decided the previous season, Patterson felt it was in his best interest to leave Kentucky a year early and apply for the NBA Draft. He was right. After graduating in three years, Patterson was one of five Kentucky players chosen in the 2010 NBA Draft—a record for any college team in one draft.

Wall was the first overall pick (a first for any Kentucky player) and went to the Washington Wizards. Cousins went fifth to the Sacramento Kings. Patterson was chosen 14th and became a Houston Rocket, alongside another former Wildcat, Chuck Hayes. Bledsoe was picked 18th by the Oklahoma City Thunder and was traded to the L.A. Clippers. Backup freshman center Daniel Orton was even chosen by the Orlando Magic, with the 29th pick.

Patterson spent some time in the NBA's Developmental League before earning a regular spot with the Rockets in March of his rookie season. He started six games, appeared in 52, and averaged almost 17 minutes, 6 points, and almost 4 rebounds a contest.

Later in the season, Patterson came back to UK to once again enjoy the crowd and his former teammates in Rupp Arena. As he took in the environment, he admitted he second-guessed himself on his decision to leave early.

"I did, it's true," he said. "I thought about what it would have been like to come back for my senior year. I want to tell these guys who are here now to have fun, because it all becomes a job when you go pro. They need to enjoy college while they can—and stay as long as they can."

# CHAPTER 32

# BRANDON KNIGHT

For outsiders watching Brandon Knight, the decision seemed like it wasn't that difficult. Since John Calipari had restored Kentucky to its rightful place among the basketball elite (only an upset to West Virginia kept the Cats out of the Final Four in 2010), Knight was able to see Calipari's track record for winning—and for sending point guards to the NBA.

There was Derrick Rose, drafted No. 1 by the Chicago Bulls. Then came Tyreke Evans, who went on to win NBA Rookie of the Year with the Sacramento Kings. John Wall followed the year after, the No. 1 overall draft pick (Kentucky's first) and the second-place finisher in voting for both the college basketball Player of the Year, then NBA Rookie of the Year.

If Knight wanted to win, and if he wanted the chance to get drafted and make money, he needed to go to one place: Kentucky. He certainly had the right attitude.

"Each day, I am trying to find a way to get better," Knight said. "Each day I am trying something to get better. Each day, everyone is trying to find something to get better at."

The only conceivable downside? Knight would have to deal with the kind of unrealistic expectations UK fans bestow upon the extremely talented.

Knight, a McDonald's All-American and the 2009 and 2010 Gatorade National Basketball Player of the Year, was a different kind of point guard—an Allen Iverson-type, cat-like quick and able to score in bunches. At 6-foot-3, he could lead your team in scoring, assists, and—as a bonus—in GPA (he was a 4.0 student in high school). He was mentally sound, and ready to become the next in line of Calipari's great point guards.

# THE SETTING

Coming off an Elite Eight run in 2010, the 2010-11 Kentucky squad was thought to be in a rebuilding year. With a second consecutive No. 1 ranked recruiting class, led by Brandon Knight, no one felt sorry for UK, but its days living at the top of the national rankings were over for a while. Newcomers Terrence Jones and Doron Lamb joined Knight, who also meshed with juniors Deandre Liggins, Darius Miller, and senior Josh Harrellson to form a crew that could be very talented. But they were not John Wall and DeMarcus Cousins and Patrick Patterson.

The season began with UK ranked No. 11, and the Wildcats won impressive games over 13th ranked Washington, 23rd ranked Notre Dame, and No. 22 Louisville in their impressive new arena, the Yum! Center. Their only losses in a nice 12-2 start were to Connecticut (and all-world point guard Kemba Walker) and at North Carolina. Not bad.

But the criticism over UK's point guard play was loud and clear. While John Wall came on the scene and dominated quickly (Wall even hit a game-winning shot in his first game), Knight was struggling to grasp his responsibilities in Calipari's offense. Knight had five turnovers in a 17-point loss to UConn, and six turnovers at Carolina. It became evident that as Brandon Knight succeeded, so would UK.

Still, Kentucky was 12-2 and ranked No. 10 in the country as it entered Southeastern Conference play. But it was then the issues of coaching a fairly young squad started to bubble to the surface. In SEC play, UK would lose six games, all away from home, all by seven points or less. In fact, three games were decided by two points, while another was decided by one point in overtime. Kentucky was favored in each, yet could not win when the game was on the line. In two games, Knight took the game winning shot, only to miss. In another, he and Lamb botched an exchange and turned the ball over.

Calipari said the team was learning how to win. But for fans, it was painful. To make matters worse, one of Knight's misses was at Florida. It was a team he wanted to beat badly—not only because it was his home state, but also because his good friend, fellow high school All-American Kenny Boynton, was a freshman star for Billy Donovan.

Knight and Kentucky came into a rematch with Florida on February 26, 2011 ranked 22nd in the nation, smarting from an overtime loss at Arkansas, and sporting a less than stellar 19-8 record, 7-6 in the SEC. In order for the Wildcats to secure a favorable seed in the NCAAs, they had to start with a win over the Gators. No one wanted it more than Knight.

What no one knew is that the Wildcats wouldn't lose again until the Final Four, more than a month later. It all started with that game at Rupp Arena against Florida.

# THE GAME OF MY LIFE
## NO. 22 KENTUCKY 76, NO. 13 FLORIDA 68
### FEBRUARY 26, 2011
### BY BRANDON KNIGHT

I think probably for us a big-time moment was when Florida came here and you know, we had lost to them before. They were the top team in the conference and we were able to beat them. We had a pretty good game overall, and I thought that was what got us rolling.

We got better since early in the season. In the beginning, we weren't as good as we thought we were. When I got here, I didn't have everything I needed to do as far as being a vocal leader. I have been able to mature in that area.

From the beginning we were always cool with each other and always happy to be around each other. But we really started to trust each other (around that time), where we really pulled together as a team to go into battle.

Darius had a really big game that night (24 points, 5 rebounds, 3 assists) and I feel like I was really steady (16 points, 6 assists, 0 turnovers) and as a team, we all just came together and we found out we could beat them. After that, we won a lot in a row.

## Statline:

| MIN | FG | FGA | 3FG | 3FGA | FT | FTA | A | TO | PTS |
|-----|----|----|-----|------|----|----|----|----|-----|
| 37 | 5 | 10 | 2 | 3 | 4 | 5 | 6 | 0 | 16 |

# THE RESULT

Kentucky went on to win 10 consecutive games. Along the way, UK won an SEC Tournament championship (defeating Florida again) earned a 4 seed in the NCAAs and marched all the way to the Final Four. Left in the wake: 21st ranked Vandy, 12th ranked Florida (twice), 22nd ranked West Virginia (in a little bit of revenge for the previous season's loss), No. 1 Ohio State and No. 7 North Carolina.

The team meshed just in time to make one of the most memorable

March runs in UK history. And during the run, the nation became to know Brandon Knight, or, as some fans came to call him, "Big Shot" Brandon.

With the game tied with a more-than-confident Princeton team in the NCAA's first round, Knight—who had not scored a point in the entire game—hit one of the biggest shots in school history when he waited for the game clock to run down, took his man off the dribble and drove to the right side of the lane. His high-arching layup kissed off the glass and fell through for the game-winner, breaking Princeton's hearts and sending the Cats to the second round.

Knight then led the Cats with 30 points in a tense win versus West Virginia in the second round. In the Sweet Sixteen, Kentucky drew No. 1 Ohio State, and in a back-and-forth game Knight again found himself with the ball in the waning seconds. After the Buckeyes drained a three to tie the game, Knight came down, shook his man to gain space, pulled up and hit a jumper with five seconds left to win the game, 62-60. In the next contest, a rematch against North Carolina, Knight poured in 22 to lead Kentucky to the Final Four, though it was Liggins who this time hit the deciding three with 37 seconds to go.

"(Brandon) is just very intelligent and a guy you like to be around," Liggins says. "No matter how he has played throughout the game you know he can make the big shots in the end."

# AFTER BLUE

Brandon Knight had one of the most memorable four games in UK history. Unfortunately, the run came to an end in a rematch against Kemba Walker and UConn in the Final Four in Houston. But man, was it close. Defensively, the Wildcats played as good as they could have, holding the Huskies to just 56 points. But UK could only muster 55.

In a Final Four when no team shot very well, the national title was there for the taking, but Knight had one of his worst outings: 6-for-23 from the field including 3-for-11 from three point land. Still, UK was right there at the end, and a missed Liggins three with time running out proved to be the difference. Of course, shooting 4-for-12 from the free throw line doesn't help, either.

Still, the run made by Kentucky was an awesome thing for a fan to watch. Winning is the most fun when it's unexpected. And few fans expected this team—the one that was once 7-6 in the conference—to make a run like this. But they did.

Afterward, UK again had to watch as its stars decided whether to stay or leave for the NBA Draft. With few great point guards to be found, Knight decided to leave—but he admitted he loved college and would love to try again for a national title.

In the 2011 NBA Draft, Knight was picked eighth overall by the Detroit Pistons, where he would join fellow Wildcat Tayshaun Prince. Now there was a new name to add to the list of great Calipari point guards: Rose, Evans, Wall—and Knight.

# CHAPTER 33

# JOSH HARRELLSON

It was a Tweet that changed Josh Harrellson's life for the better—even though it didn't seem like it at first.

Harrellson was lucky just to be on UK's team, really. A 6-10 center with bulk who could shoot, Harrellson was a junior college player from Missouri who came to Kentucky under the Billy Gillispie regime. Harrellson only started playing basketball as a freshman in high school. He quickly became a fan favorite at UK because of his quirky personality (he received the nickname Jorts for his tendency to wear jean-shorts, and he loved the attention). When John Calipari took the UK job, many thought Harrellson would be let go. But Calipari saw something in Harrellson. Maybe he liked how the guy could shoot. Maybe he liked how he was one of the few big players on the team.

Whatever the reason, Harrellson was allowed to remain a Wildcat. In the star-studded year of 2010, he had to watch as more talented players took all the minutes. In 2011, his senior year, many fans thought the same thing was going to happen. Even Harrellson himself was not counting on much playing time.

Why? Two words: Enes Kanter.

Kanter, a 6-11 player from Turkey, wanted to play collegiately at Kentucky. Many thought he was so talented he would be the No. 1 player chosen in the NBA Draft if he were to declare. But in a twist of fate, the NCAA ruled that Kanter could not play collegiate basketball due to his taking thousands of dollars when playing for a professional team overseas.

So the big man UK was supposed to have on campus? He was gone. And who would get to start in his place? Josh Harrellson.

The friction started in the preseason Blue/White scrimmage, when

UK players compete against themselves in front of fans. Harrellson played hard and well, pulling down 26 rebounds. When Calipari was asked about his center's performance, the coach did not offer a lot of praise, instead admitting that the scrimmage was nothing more than a glorified practice.

Harrellson did not react well. He went to his public Twitter account. "It's just amazing to me I can't get a good job or a way to go," Harrellson tweeted. "But I look past it and keep trucking. You can't stop this train."

Calipari responded with the understatement that Harrellson did not handle success very well. Then the coach suspended Harrellson's Twitter privileges and put the player on an early morning running regimen. The discipline, mixed with the added cardio, transformed Josh Harrellson.

# THE SETTING

Even though Enes Kanter was not allowed to play, he was allowed to practice with the team. And every day, Harrellson had to play against an NBA-ready center with better moves than most any other center Harrellson would face in college.

"It helps a lot," Harrellson said during the season. "Going against (Kanter) everyday makes me a better player. Every day in and out just competing against him, doing drills with him, even if I am not going against him just watching him; I am just trying to match him. Just doing that makes me more confident and being able to stop him in practice make me go into every game knowing I am not going to play someone as good as Enes."

It was the Louisville game that really served as Harrellson's coming-out party. The Cardinals approached the game with one idea: To not let freshman forward Terrence Jones beat them. Instead, they forgot about (or possibly just did not know) Josh Harrellson, who went for 23 points and 14 rebounds in a 15-point win over the Cards. In the final moments, he walked off the court and ran into the arms of Calipari, who bear-hugged the player.

Throughout the season, Harrellson would anchor the middle, finishing second in the SEC in rebounding (to teammate Terrence Jones). He also kept at the running, even after Calipari told him he could quit. But never would his presence make more of a difference than on UK's surprising road to the Final Four. In the Wildcats' upset win over No. 1 Ohio State in the Sweet Sixteen, Harrellson stood toe to-toe with Buckeye All-American freshman Jared Sullinger, scoring 17 points and grabbing 10 rebounds. (Sullinger had 21 and 16). Harrellson used his athleticism and shooting ability to make the Ohio State big man chase him all over the court. And Harrellson was not intimidated; on one play, the UK center saved a ball by catching it in mi-air and heaving it back to Sullinger, slamming it off his body and out of bounds. The move was bold and forceful – and Sullinger looked like he could not believe someone would do that to him.

"Josh has been a big inspiration for each and every one of us and it just shows us that if you work hard, and you put your mind to it, you can get better and help our team where we really need it, inside," Brandon Knight said.

The UK win would send them to a rematch of an earlier game with North Carolina.tThis time a spot in the Final Four was on the line.

It was the biggest game of Harrellson's career.

# THE GAME OF MY LIFE
## NCAA REGIONAL FINALS
## NO. 11 KENTUCKY 76, NO. 7 NORTH CAROLINA 69
### MARCH 27, 2011
### BY JOSH HARRELLSON

Just getting to the Final Four, making it one step further than last year's team and going out my senior year with a bang, it's amazing. I have always had a work ethic, but I really didn't use it much my first two years here. (The coaching staff) brought it out of me this year and I have worked so hard. I plan on working this hard till I am done playing.

It is a complete 180 (from last year). Last year I didn't play at all, I just sat and watched. It was still fun though because we were 35-3. This year has just been a dream come true, playing significant minutes, helping my teammates win games that I never thought I could do and it has been a great ride.

Against North Carolina we got up by double digits and we just seemed to be hitting every big shot we needed, or getting every big rebound. And then they came back, and they just started doing the same thing. They have so much talent, we were just hanging on there at the end and then (Liggins) hit the big three to clinch it for us. We were all jumping around after that. It was so much fun. It made everything worth it.

## STATLINE:

| MIN | FG | FGA | FT | FTA | REB | A | B | S | PTS |
|-----|----|----|----|----|----|----|----|----|-----|
| 38 | 4 | 6 | 4 | 7 | 8 | 4 | 1 | 2 | 12 |

# THE RESULT

Harrellson helped lead Kentucky to its first Final Four appearance in 13 years. And to make it even sweeter for UK fans, the Cats were able to defeat a hated rival on the way to the National Semifinals. Even after their eventual loss to Connecticut in the Final Four, Jorts and the Wildcats found a special place in the hearts of UK fans everywhere.

In a rebuilding season, when Kentucky lost its best post player to an NCAA ruling, Harrellson stepped up and played like an All-American.

And it paid off in the end.

# AFTER BLUE

In a surprise to many across the nation, in 2011 Josh Harrellson was drafted in the second round by the NBA's New Orleans Hornets, but then was traded to the New York Knicks. His performance in his senior year, coupled with his outstanding NCAA Tournament, earned him a shot in the NBA.

For what it's worth, Enes Kanter was drafted No. 3 overall by the Utah Jazz.

The pair will be forever linked in UK lore. Someday, if they happen to meet on an NBA court, you know the two will shake hands, reminisce and think back to when Harrellson finally reached his potential.

# ACKNOWLEDGMENTS

Thanks first to all those players who were so eager to speak about their most memorable games. Without their cooperation, this project would not exist. Thanks also to the University of Kentucky Sports Information staff, especially Scott Stricklin, who researched many old newspaper articles on certain games and always helped get me into places I couldn't have found on my own.

To Jon Scott and his web-based UK historical archive, I am forever grateful (find it at www.bigbluehistory.net/bb/wildcats.html). To Dick Weiss (with Rick Pitino), Billy Reed (with Cawood Ledford), Tom Wallace, Gregg Doyel, and Denny Trease, your books on the subject were invaluable. To Pat Crowley, as well as my friends and fellow fanatics Joe and Julie Cox, thanks for watching my back. To Shannon Russell, thank you for helping me find my way around Rupp Arena. To Dave Niinemets, thanks for taking me to the mall to help do what most opponents could not: Slow down Patrick Sparks. To my friends Jerry Tipton and Jerry Brewer, thanks for helping me navigate the public relations world of the NBA. And to those NBA public relations personnel and agents I spoke with, my eternal gratitude.

To Dick Vitale, thank you for taking time out of your busy schedule—during dinner, no less—to talk about your favorite UK game. You talked to me when other celebrities, some of whom call themselves Kentucky fans, would not.

And to John Humenik, Doug Hoepker, and everyone at Sports Publishing, thank you for the opportunity.

To my former employers at *The Cincinnati Enquirer*, thank you for allowing me to pursue the book.

And, to my family—this project took time away from them. While I was having fun, they were missing me. My thanks to them most of all.